Sailing Upside Down: The Clandestine Politics of Affluence and Malfeasance

CHANDRA PRAKASH

Sailing Upside Down

The Clandestine Politics of Affluence and Malfeasance

First edition

Published 2024

ISBN :

Type set by

Printed /

Published by

Chandra Prakash

Email

inquiries or feedback

12cp19@gmail.com
sailingupsidedown19@gmail.com

+91 7302231412

Contents

1. The Mirage of Virtue: Wealth's Hidden Agenda

Explores the deceptive nature of virtue often
associated with affluence. It reveals how the wealthy
mask their true intentions under the guise of
philanthropy, ultimately perpetuating systems of power
and control.

**2. Invisible Hands: The Subterranean Forces Behind the
Glittering Façade**

Unseen forces financial, political, and social are
dissected in this chapter, which exposes the
subterranean networks that work to uphold the visible
glamour of wealth, while operating in the shadows to
shape global systems.

**3. The Currency of Influence: How Wealth Shapes
Policy and Perception**

Examines the profound influence of wealth on politics,
revealing how the powerful use their resources not only
to dictate policy but to shape public perception,
ensuring their dominance in every sphere of society.

**4. Veils of Deception: The Politics of Accountability and
Evasion**

Explore the complex political strategies employed by
the elite to evade accountability for their actions.
Through a web of manipulation, they deflect

responsibility while maintaining their grip on power and wealth.

5. Illusion of Choice: How Wealth Dictates Freedom

The concept of freedom is redefined as the chapter explores how wealth shapes the options available to individuals. What appears as personal choice is often a controlled, constrained process dictated by the powerful forces of money and influence.

6. The Masters of Puppets: The Global Reach of Wealth and Power

We trace the global reach of wealth and power, showing how a small elite pulls the strings on international policies, conflicts, and economies, orchestrating events from behind the curtain to maintain their supremacy.

7. The Architecture of Illusion: How Wealth Designs Perception and Reality

Wealth doesn't just buy material goods—it constructs reality itself. This chapter looks at how the affluent class uses media, culture, and technology to design and control the narratives that define societal norms and individual desires.

8. Empire of Consumption: How Desire Is Engineered

Examines the mechanics of consumerism, showing how the desires of individuals are manipulated and manufactured by corporations and the wealthy elite to fuel a cycle of perpetual consumption that benefits the powerful.

9. Cartography of Containment: How Wealth Constructs and Dismantles Resistance

At the crossroads of power and geography, wealth becomes both the architect and the destroyer of resistance. This chapter maps how economic dominance shapes societal boundaries and stifles collective efforts to resist.

10. The Specter of Erosion: How Wealth Corrodes the Fabric of Justice

In the shadow of affluence, justice withers away. Here, we investigate how the corrosive influence of wealth dismantles the integrity of legal and ethical systems, fostering inequality at every level.

11. The Alchemy of Illusion: Transforming Moral Decay into Virtue

Through the lens of alchemical transformation, this chapter examines the seductive process by which society turns moral decay into a guise of virtue, masking the rot beneath with the appearance of righteousness.

12. Mirage of Stability: How Wealth Manufactures the Illusion of Order

Delving into the false narratives that sustain order, we uncover how the powerful engineer the illusion of stability, distracting from the fragile, often precarious reality they create for the masses.

13. Dystopia of Desire: How Wealth Engineers the Longing for Subjugation

Desire becomes a tool of control as wealth cultivates a culture of longing not for freedom, but for subjugation. This chapter examines how economic forces channel desire into compliance with the status quo.

14. The Erosion of Collective Consciousness: How History is Rewritten for Power's Sake

History is malleable in the hands of the powerful. This chapter explores how those in power distort collective memory to serve their interests, erasing or rewriting history to solidify their control over the present.

15. Tyranny of Convenience: How Ease and Efficiency Breed Dependency

Convenience, once a marker of progress, becomes a tool of tyranny. Here, we explore how a culture obsessed with efficiency fosters dependency, rendering individuals and societies vulnerable to control.

16. The Spectacle of Existence: How Society's Obsession with Appearances Eclipses Substance

In a world dominated by spectacle, appearances reign supreme. This chapter critiques society's shallow fixation on image over essence, where the pursuit of superficial recognition overshadows deeper truths.

17. The Fragmentation of Reality: The Collapse of Consensus and the Death of Truth

As truth becomes increasingly elusive, reality itself fractures. This chapter unravels the collapse of shared consensus, tracing the origins and consequences of a world in which truth has become a casualty of ideological warfare.

18. The Illusion of Progress: How Technological Utopianism Conceals the Dystopia Beneath

Beneath the glossy promises of technological advancement lies a darker reality. This chapter exposes how the vision of a technological utopia often conceals a lurking dystopia that exploits the very progress it promises.

19. Specter of Inequality: How the System Perpetuates Itself

Inequality is no mere byproduct; it is an integral cog in the machinery of power. Here, we explore how systemic inequality is perpetuated by design, maintaining the status quo and reinforcing the privileges of the few.

20. The Anatomy of Control: How Power Manipulates the Masses

Control is both an art and a science. In this chapter, we dissect the intricate mechanisms through which power manipulates the masses—shaping thoughts, behaviors, and ideologies to consolidate authority.

21. Spectacle of Consent: How Power Manufactures Compliance

Consent is no longer freely given but carefully engineered. This chapter delves into the sophisticated processes through which power manufactures compliance, ensuring the silent acquiescence of the populace.

22. The Alchemy of Obscurity: How Information is Weaponized

Information, once a pillar of knowledge, is now a weapon in the hands of the powerful. This chapter unpacks how information is deliberately obscured or distorted to control perception and shape public opinion.

23. The Mirage of Sovereignty: How Power Alters Perception of Freedom

Freedom, in the hands of the powerful, is often nothing more than an illusion. This chapter examines how sovereignty is redefined and manipulated to shape our perception of liberty while subtly limiting true autonomy.

24. The Surrender of Autonomy: How The Mind Becomes The Final Battleground

The battle for freedom no longer takes place in the streets but in the mind. Here, we explore the subtle psychological warfare that undermines individual autonomy, turning the mind into the final frontier of control.

25. Unseen Hand: The Quiet Revolution of Corporatocracy

While revolutions are traditionally loud and violent, the rise of corporatocracy is a silent coup. This chapter investigates how corporate interests quietly revolutionize governance, exerting power behind the scenes.

26. The Alchemy of Control: How The Fabric of Society is Woven With Threads of Deception

Control is not merely imposed but woven into the very fabric of society. This chapter reveals how deception serves as the thread that holds the social order together, maintaining equilibrium through manipulation.

27. The Tyranny of the Status Quo: How Comfort and Complacency Sustain the System

The comfort of the status quo breeds complacency, allowing tyranny to thrive. This chapter explores how societal inertia, bolstered by a false sense of security, sustains oppressive systems that resist change.

28. Echoes of Empire: How History's Ghosts Continue to Shape Our Present

Empires may have fallen, but their ghosts continue to haunt the present. In this chapter, we explore how the legacies of imperialism continue to shape global dynamics, from politics to culture, long after their formal end.

29. The Threshold of Awakening: A World on the Edge

Humanity stands at the precipice of profound change. This chapter examines the threshold of awakening, where the world teeters between continuing apathy and an emerging global consciousness.

Reckoning of Silence: Confronting the Empire Within True liberation begins within. This chapter calls for an introspective reckoning with the silence that sustains internalized forms of empire and oppression, urging individuals to confront the forces that shape their beliefs.

Labyrinth of Self: Awakening to the Infinite The journey of awakening is not linear but labyrinthine. In this final chapter, we explore the intricate journey of self-discovery, where individuals transcend the ego and awaken to the infinite possibilities of consciousness and being.

Preface

In a world where prosperity often disguises itself as virtue and power cloaks itself in righteousness, the delicate dance of affluence and malfeasance remains one of the most insidious and paradoxical aspects of contemporary society. *Sailing Upside Down: The Clandestine Politics of Affluence and Malfeasance* seeks to unravel this tangled web, probing beneath the polished veneers of affluence and unraveling the machinations that often go unnoticed by the very systems that glorify them.

This work is not merely an expose it is an interrogation of the systems, ideologies, and individual actors that shape a society where the opulent sail unscathed, their vessels steering ever higher, while the wreckage of deceit and corruption lies hidden beneath the surface. Through meticulous analysis and a daring exploration of the murky intersections of wealth, power, and ethical decay, this book seeks to shine a light on the covert dynamics that enable the affluent to manipulate the very structures designed to ensure accountability.

The title, *Sailing Upside Down*, evokes not just the irony inherent in the subject matter, but the inherent dissonance that governs the relationship between wealth and power. To sail upside down is to disregard the conventional laws of nature and ethics, charting a course where societal norms are upended, and the line between right and wrong becomes dangerously blurred.

In these pages, I invite the reader to embark on a journey that will challenge preconceived notions, provoke introspection, and, perhaps most importantly, instigate a dialogue on the price of affluence and the cost of its malfeasance. The politics of affluence are far from transparent, and the machinery of corruption often remains shrouded in secrecy; yet, within these shadows lies the truth if we dare to look.

Through this exploration, I aim not only to dissect the tangled politics of wealth and malfeasance but also to encourage a broader understanding of the consequences these forces have on our social fabric, our institutions, and our very notion of justice. As we chart a course through these waters, I urge the reader to question the very foundation upon which our system of power and privilege is built, for the sailing, in truth, is anything but straight.

CHANDRA PRAKASH   **December 2024**

One

The Mirage of Virtue: Wealth's Hidden Agenda

In the grand theatre of human history, few phenomena have been as omnipresent and yet as elusive as the intricate relationship between wealth and virtue. To the untrained eye, the affluent are often draped in the regalia of righteousness, their fortunes seemingly borne of industriousness, merit, and benevolent intention. Yet, beneath the gleaming surface of this gilded facade lies a far murkier truth a web of moral equivocation, self-interest, and, at times, insidious malfeasance that governs the world of affluence.

Wealth, it seems, is a master of deception. Its ability to cloak itself in the illusion of virtue is perhaps its most pernicious trait. The monied elite, perched atop their carefully constructed citadels of power, often justify their privilege by invoking the rhetoric of self-made success, ethical capitalism, or charitable endeavor. The veritable high priests of the free market, they claim their affluence as the product of hard work, ingenuity, and an adherence to principles of meritocracy that, in truth, often serve as little more than smoke and mirrors. Beneath this outward projection of rectitude lies a hidden agenda one that is not simply interested in the preservation of wealth, but in the maintenance of a carefully constructed narrative that perpetuates inequality under the guise of moral superiority.

The myth of the self-made millionaire is perhaps the most enduring and dangerous of these narratives. It suggests that wealth is solely the result of individual merit, obscuring the far more complex and, at times, nefarious processes that contribute to the amassing of vast fortunes. The billionaire, draped in the trappings of entrepreneurship and social responsibility, becomes a paragon of virtuous success. Yet, this image of the solitary innovator, unswerving in their commitment to the common good, belies the countless compromises, exploitations, and subversions that characterize the true path to affluence. To accept the myth of meritocracy is to turn a blind eye to the entrenched systems of privilege and power that enable the rich to remain rich, often at the expense of those who labor beneath them.

In this context, wealth becomes more than a mere accumulation of capital it becomes a vehicle for the manipulation of societal structures. It is a force that reshapes the very fabric of governance, law, and morality to ensure its perpetuation. The powerful, cloaked in the garb of philanthropy and corporate responsibility, are frequently the architects of the very systems of exploitation that enable them to thrive. Tax shelters, offshore accounts, regulatory loopholes, and corporate lobbying are but a few of the tools in their arsenal tools that are wielded with the precision of a master craftsman, designed not to benefit the common good, but to fortify the positions of those already at the top.

The charitable endeavors of the wealthy, often presented as benevolent acts of altruism, are frequently imbued with far more complexity. Philanthropy, in this context, is not merely an expression of goodwill, but a strategic maneuver one that serves to bolster the status and influence of the donor while simultaneously deflecting attention from the systemic inequalities that their wealth perpetuates. The donation of millions to ostensibly noble causes is not simply an act of generosity but a calculated effort to create a public persona that is untouchable, virtuous, and, perhaps most importantly, immune to scrutiny. In this way, wealth, through its veneer of virtue, shields itself from the moral questions that might otherwise arise.

What is often obscured in the fog of this virtuous façade is the true cost of affluence the price paid by those who exist in the periphery of these grand narratives. For every philanthropic gesture, there are multitudes whose labor is exploited, whose rights are trampled, and whose futures are dictated by the whims of those who command great fortune. The wealth that is amassed at the apex of society is rarely the product of isolated genius or fortuitous circumstance; it is the result of a complex interplay of historical exploitation, structural inequality, and strategic manipulation. And yet, those who possess this wealth have cultivated an environment where their moral agency remains beyond reproach, and their responsibility to the society from which they profit is conveniently obfuscated.

To navigate the labyrinth of wealth's hidden agenda is to confront the uncomfortable truth that affluence, far from being an innocent byproduct of talent or effort, is often the product of systemic malfeasance. It is to understand that the gilded narratives surrounding the rich and powerful are not mere stories, but strategic constructs designed to obscure the mechanisms of control, subjugation, and manipulation. In the words of the philosopher, the first step toward enlightenment is the willingness to see beyond illusion. To gaze through the mirage of virtue and recognize the hidden agenda of affluence is to understand that wealth is not simply a measure of success, but a tool one that is wielded to shape the political, economic, and social landscapes of our world.

The challenge, therefore, is not merely to critique the wealthy and their machinations, but to dismantle the very systems that enable their wealth to flourish unchecked. It is to deconstruct the myth of meritocracy and expose the moral and political decay that underpins the edifice of affluence. For as long as wealth is allowed to masquerade as virtue, the powerful will continue to sail, unchallenged, upon seas of inequality, their agendas hidden in plain sight.

Two

Invisible Hands: The Subterranean Forces Behind the Glittering Facade

Behind every towering skyscraper of wealth, beneath the gilded veneer of corporate success, there exists a network of unseen forces subterranean currents that quietly shape the world of affluence and power. These invisible hands, elusive yet omnipotent, orchestrate the grand narratives of prosperity while remaining beyond the reach of scrutiny. They are the architects of systems that appear transparent and just, yet are, in reality, deeply entrenched in exploitation, manipulation, and corruption.

In the surface-level rhetoric of capitalism, the narrative is one of merit and reward. The marketplace is presented as an arena where skill, innovation, and tenacity determine success. The wealthy, in this narrative, are champions of a system that values hard work and individual genius. Yet this is a myth an elegant illusion crafted by those whose interests lie in maintaining the status quo. The reality is that wealth does not accrue through individual endeavor alone, but through a labyrinthine system of covert transactions, collusion, and systemic inequities, all facilitated by invisible hands working in concert to maintain the facade.

These forces are not abstract; they are the well-oiled mechanisms of power that operate in the shadows of legislation, in the corridors of corporate boardrooms, and in the encrypted messages exchanged across global financial networks. They are the policymakers whose influence ensures that tax loopholes persist, the lobbyists who shape the laws to benefit the few at the expense of the many, and the multinational corporations whose reach extends far beyond borders, circumventing regulations with impunity. The wealth that is displayed so prominently in the public sphere is the product of a vast, subterranean economy an economy that operates on the margins of legality, ethics, and transparency.

Consider the network of financial institutions that forms the backbone of global wealth. In the visible world, banks are presented as paragons of stability, places where the prudent and the industrious come to safeguard their futures. Yet beneath the polished surface lies a realm of complex financial instruments derivatives, offshore accounts, and shadow markets that allow the wealthy to shield their assets from scrutiny, evade taxes, and exert undue influence over public policy. These invisible hands direct the flow of capital, making it possible for vast fortunes to multiply while the vast majority remain ensnared in a web of economic precarity. This subterranean economy, with its opaque mechanisms and its untouchable elite, is one of the principal forces that maintains the illusion of equality in a world profoundly shaped by inequality.

One of the most insidious elements of these invisible forces is their ability to shape public perception. The narrative of success, so carefully cultivated by the wealthy, is not just a marketing tool; it is an ideological construct. It is a belief system designed to justify the existing power structures, to convince the populace that the economic disparities of society are natural, inevitable, and even righteous. This is the work of think tanks, media moguls, and social influencers agents of ideological warfare who create the very frameworks through which the masses interpret wealth and power. Through the manipulation of information, the subtle crafting of consent, and the dissemination of ideas that privilege the interests of the wealthy, these invisible hands ensure that the status quo remains largely unquestioned.

The corporate titans who appear to operate independently, making decisions based on rational market forces, are in fact participants in a system that thrives on collusion, secrecy, and the erosion of competition. Monopolies, oligopolies, and cartels unseen by the average consumer dominate industries across the globe. From tech giants to energy conglomerates, these entities shape the market according to their will, consolidating power and wealth in ways that are invisible to the public eye. What is presented as competition is often an elaborate game of preordained outcomes, where the players, though appearing diverse, are in fact coordinated under the influence of a few shadowy figures and institutions.

But the subterranean forces behind the glittering façade are not confined to the private sector. The state itself is a participant in this complex dance of power, wealth, and manipulation. Governments, ostensibly the protectors of public interest, are often beholden to the same forces that fuel corporate power. The revolving door between high-ranking government officials and corporate executives creates a seamless flow of influence and information, blurring the lines between public service and private profit. Policies are crafted not in the interests of the people, but to sustain the interests of the few. The invisible hands of wealth direct the course of political action, ensuring that public resources are allocated in ways that perpetuate the cycle of inequality.

At the heart of this system is an economic philosophy that privileges accumulation over equity, exploitation over fairness, and power over justice. The global financial system, with its intricate web of debt, capital flows, and speculative investments, ensures that the wealthy retain control over the levers of power. For every new skyscraper that rises, there is an invisible hand manipulating the financial instruments that made it possible. For every charity that receives a donation from a billionaire, there are the unspoken consequences of the policies and practices that allowed that wealth to be amassed in the first place.

The real power of these invisible hands lies in their ability to remain undetected, to operate in the shadows while their impact is felt on every facet of society. The wealthy, secure behind their curtains of opacity, continue to shape the world according to their interests, while the masses remain distracted by the dazzling displays of affluence and the hollow promises of meritocracy. To confront the true nature of this system is to peer into a darkness that few are willing to acknowledge. It requires an understanding of the deep entanglements of wealth, power, and corruption a recognition that the façade of prosperity is not the result of individual achievement, but the consequence of a carefully constructed, and ruthlessly maintained, order.

Three

The Currency of Influence: How Wealth Shapes Policy and Perception

In the complex matrix of modern governance, where the lines between politics, economy, and culture have become increasingly blurred, one immutable truth remains: wealth is the most potent currency of influence. Its power extends far beyond the material accumulation of goods and services it is a force that shapes ideologies, molds policy, and dictates the very framework within which public perception is crafted. Those who wield wealth do not merely accumulate capital; they shape the world in their image, ensuring that their interests remain paramount, while the mechanisms of democracy and governance bend to their will.

Wealth, as a currency, operates on a multidimensional plane. It is, at its most fundamental level, the instrument of control. But it is also a medium of persuasion, an asset that buys not only resources but also the allegiance of those who are entrusted with power. Through its invisible hand, wealth infiltrates every aspect of the policymaking process, from the drafting of legislation to the formation of public opinion. What is often obscured in the cacophony of political discourse is the extent to which financial elites influence the decisions that ostensibly belong to the public sphere. The modern state, far from being the impartial arbiter of justice, has become a servant to the forces of affluence its policies crafted in boardrooms rather than town halls, its mandates shaped by the highest bidder rather than the majority vote.

At the heart of this currency of influence lies a network of strategic investments financial, social, and intellectual that ensures the elite remain in control. In the corridors of power, a select few understand the true mechanics of influence: it is not simply a matter of donating to political campaigns, but of shaping the very structure of decision-making itself. Corporate lobbyists, with their finely honed expertise, navigate the complexities of legislation with a precision that far exceeds the capabilities of the average policymaker. Their ability to craft favorable policy, bypass regulatory hurdles, and ensure that the interests of the wealthy are embedded within the legal framework is a testament to the pervasive reach of wealth.

These lobbyists are but the public face of a much more insidious network of influence that extends through think tanks, advisory committees, and consulting firms institutions that operate at the intersection of academia, politics, and business. Here, the rich and powerful do not merely fund campaigns; they fund ideas. The ideologies that permeate modern governance are often not the product of democratic discourse, but of strategic investments in intellectual infrastructure designed to maintain the status quo. Think tanks, masquerading as neutral policy advisers, are, in reality, breeding grounds for the propagation of pro-corporate, pro-wealth narratives that are then seamlessly woven into the fabric of public policy. These ideas, presented as the product of unbiased research, have the dual function of legitimizing the existing economic order while simultaneously obscuring the structures of inequality that underpin it.

The influence of wealth extends beyond the formal mechanisms of policy-making and into the realm of public perception an equally important battleground where the narratives of affluence and

power are contested. Public opinion, it turns out, is
not as organic or as democratic as it appears.
Rather, it is the product of sophisticated media
strategies, carefully calibrated advertisements, and
strategically placed stories that shape the way
society views wealth, power, and governance. The
wealthiest individuals and corporations understand
that perception is not just reality it is the
foundation of control. Through their investments in
media conglomerates, advertising firms, and public
relations agencies, the rich have created a system
of information warfare designed to reinforce their
dominance.

Consider the role of the media in shaping public
perception of wealth and power. The same media
outlets that report on the opulent lifestyles of the
rich are often the very ones that obscure the
mechanisms of their affluence. Through carefully
curated narratives, the media perpetuates the
myth of the self-made billionaire, framing their
success as a testament to ingenuity and
perseverance, while disregarding the systemic
advantages that undergird their rise. Corporate
sponsors, major shareholders, and influential
figures sit at the helm of media networks, ensuring

that their interests are represented in the stories that are told to the public. The media, rather than serving as a fourth estate, has become an extension of the corporate empire, shaping discourse in ways that serve the interests of the few, while silencing dissenting voices.

At the intersection of wealth and perception lies a critical tool in the arsenal of the powerful: branding. The process of branding is, in essence, the manipulation of perception transforming a company, an individual, or a political cause into something more than a commodity, but rather an ideology. Through branding, the wealthy create narratives that transcend the immediate material benefits of their products or services, instead cultivating an emotional connection with consumers and citizens alike.

The billionaire philanthropist is not just a wealthy individual; they are a symbol of compassion, of progress, of social responsibility. The corporation is not just a profit-driven entity; it is a champion of innovation, a harbinger of positive change. The power of branding lies in its ability to transform the most self-interested motives into public virtues, making it possible for the affluent to wield influence under the guise of altruism.

In the political arena, the same dynamics of branding are at play. Politicians, many of whom owe their rise to the largesse of wealthy donors, adopt the rhetoric and strategies of their benefactors. They sell themselves not as public servants, but as champions of the same neoliberal ideology that underpins corporate hegemony. Elections become spectacles of wealth, with the candidates most adept at brand-building at curating the right image becoming the most successful. It is not enough to be right; one must appear right, embody the right values, and present oneself as aligned with the ideals of the electorate. In this world, perception is the true currency, and it is bought and sold at the highest price.

Ultimately, the currency of influence reveals the most insidious truth of all: that the political and economic systems in which we participate are not designed to serve the collective good, but to perpetuate the interests of a small, powerful elite. Wealth, far from being a tool of personal success, becomes a tool of structural control a force that shapes not just policies but entire worldviews, altering the very way in which society understands justice, merit, and equality. Through its insidious manipulation of policy and perception, the wealthy ensure that the game remains rigged in their favor, their power entrenched not through force, but through the subtler, more pervasive mechanisms of influence.

Four

Veils of Deception: The Politics of Accountability and Evasion

In the grand theatre of political governance and corporate influence, the most insidious of performances are those veiled in deception where accountability is an illusion and evasion, a masterstroke of strategy. Beneath the surface of legalese, moral arguments, and public-facing ideals, the powerful weave a complex tapestry designed not only to obscure their own culpability but to deflect scrutiny from the systemic engines that perpetuate inequality and malfeasance. In this labyrinth of misdirection, the architects of wealth and power play their part with chilling precision, maintaining the appearance of virtue while their actions are often steeped in exploitation and manipulation.

The very notion of accountability the idea that those who wield power should be held responsible for their actions has become a mockery, a hollow concept in a world where wealth and influence are the ultimate safeguards against consequence. For the elite, accountability is a malleable construct, shaped not by the demands of justice but by the constraints of public opinion and the dexterity with which they can navigate the legal and political landscapes. What we witness is not an honest reckoning of power, but an elaborate theatre of appearances, where the act of accountability is performed for the public eye, while the true levers of control remain firmly in the hands of the wealthy.

This performance begins with the creation of institutions designed to safeguard the powerful, cloaked in the illusion of impartiality and due process. Regulatory bodies, watchdog organizations, and legal frameworks, which were ostensibly created to ensure transparency and fairness, have instead become tools of control. The very agencies tasked with holding the powerful accountable have, over time, been co-opted by the forces of wealth, ensuring that they function not as instruments of justice, but as mechanisms of evasion. These institutions, once conceived as checks on corporate and governmental excess, now serve as vehicles for obfuscation, enabling the elite to craft their own narratives of innocence and merit.

The mechanisms of evasion are varied and multifaceted, yet they all share a singular characteristic: a relentless pursuit of delay and distraction. The legal system, for example, is a prime tool in the arsenal of the powerful, who have the resources to prolong litigation indefinitely, rendering justice an elusive goal. High-priced lawyers, an army of consultants, and a network of sympathetic judges create a web of legal complexity that ensures accountability is constantly deferred. For those with wealth, the cost of justice is often so prohibitive that they can afford to delay, distort, and obfuscate until public attention wanes, leaving them free to continue their machinations unscathed.

The corporate world operates with similarly sophisticated tactics of evasion. When malfeasance is exposed, the response is often not one of genuine reform or reparation, but of calculated damage control. The use of public relations firms, spin doctors, and media manipulation ensures that the focus remains on the appearance of corporate responsibility, not its actual practices. Scandals are framed as isolated incidents, individual errors in judgment rather than systemic flaws. Corporate social responsibility programs are rolled out, offering paltry gestures of goodwill, while the root causes of exploitation remain unaddressed. The message to the public is clear: we are sorry, but we are not guilty.

But it is not only in the legal and corporate spheres that the politics of evasion thrive. The political landscape, too, is a carefully crafted illusion where accountability is consistently thwarted by the very institutions meant to ensure democratic integrity. Election cycles, which should serve as opportunities for the public to hold their leaders accountable, are instead transformed into elaborate spectacles of wealth and influence. Political campaigns, fueled by vast sums of money, are no longer about competing visions of the future, but about whose financial backing can create the most persuasive image. The very concept of "accountability" is reduced to a PR campaign, where the wealthy and powerful can buy their way into public office and, once there, continue to serve the interests of their benefactors.

At the highest levels of power, the evasion of accountability is institutionalized. The revolving door between corporate boardrooms and government positions ensures that those who make the rules are often the same people who benefit from them. Politicians become executives, executives become regulators, and the cycle perpetuates itself, creating an unbreakable nexus of power that shields the elite from scrutiny. The regulatory frameworks that are supposed to keep corporate excess in check are instead designed with loopholes that allow for the unimpeded flow of capital. The law becomes an instrument not of justice, but of convenience, ensuring that those in power remain untouchable while the disadvantaged are left to bear the burdens of a system that is rigged from the outset.

This culture of evasion is further entrenched by the strategic use of distraction. In a world saturated with information, the elite know that keeping the public's attention diverted is key to maintaining the status quo. Media spectacles, celebrity scandals, and manufactured crises serve to divert public scrutiny from the true sources of power and corruption. Meanwhile, the real decisions are made in boardrooms, in legislative chambers, and in financial hubs, far from the prying eyes of the public. The power to shape public opinion through controlled narratives, be it through media, advertising, or political messaging, ensures that the actions of the powerful are seen not for what they are, but for what those in control wish them to be perceived as.

Yet, perhaps the most profound tool of evasion is the manipulation of public conscience itself. Through a calculated and relentless bombardment of propaganda, the wealthy and powerful have succeeded in altering the way we think about wealth, inequality, and power. The narrative of meritocracy so deeply ingrained in the modern psyche has become a shield behind which the elite can hide. The myth of the self-made billionaire, the story of success earned through hard work and ingenuity, serves to justify the accumulation of vast fortunes, while obscuring the systemic exploitation that underpins it. Those who dare to challenge this narrative, who point to the ways in which the powerful evade responsibility, are cast aside as radicals, enemies of the system, and threats to the social order.

Ultimately, the politics of accountability and evasion are not just about individual acts of malfeasance, but about a systemic failure a failure to address the deep inequalities embedded in the structures of power. The veils of deception are not merely a series of tactics, but a reflection of a deeper truth: that the systems we rely on for justice, for fairness, and for accountability are themselves compromised. The powerful have learned to navigate these systems with such precision that they remain largely immune to the consequences of their actions. And in this immunity, they perpetuate the cycle of inequality, ensuring that accountability remains an elusive, ever-distant ideal.

Five

The Illusion of Choice: How Wealth Dictates Freedom

In a world where the rhetoric of democracy, freedom, and equality pervades every corner of the political and economic landscape, it is essential to interrogate the true nature of the choices we believe we have. The foundational tenets of modern societies proclaim that choice is the epitome of freedom that individuals, unshackled from coercion, can navigate their destinies through their decisions. Yet beneath the glossy veneer of this purported autonomy lies an insidious truth: the choices we make, far from being manifestations of free will, are meticulously engineered and circumscribed by the invisible but omnipotent hand of wealth. In this paradigm, the affluent do not merely accumulate capital; they manufacture consent, sculpt desires, and dictate the boundaries within which individual freedom is permitted to operate.

The illusion of choice is the most sophisticated and pervasive form of control ever devised. It operates not through overt coercion, but through the subtle manipulation of options the creation of a simulacrum of freedom that appears, on the surface, to empower the individual, while in reality, it entrenches the power of the few. Wealth, in this context, does not merely buy influence; it constructs the very framework within which choices are made. The affluent, with their vast reserves of capital, do not just secure their own futures; they shape the very structures of opportunity, steering the public's options into channels that ultimately serve their interests. This manufactured landscape of choice serves to pacify the masses, to convince them that their destinies lie in their own hands, even as the true architects of their fate remain hidden behind the curtain of affluence.

To understand how wealth dictates freedom, one must first grasp the underlying mechanisms that govern the marketplace of ideas and opportunities. In the economic sphere, the illusion of choice is most starkly illustrated in the realm of consumerism. Advertisements, branding, and media narratives bombard the individual with an overwhelming array of choices each promising a form of self-expression, individuality, or empowerment. Yet, in this vast sea of options, the true diversity of choice is an illusion. The brands that dominate the market are not the result of meritocratic competition, but of monopolistic control and strategic consolidation. The consumer is presented with a dazzling array of superficial choices, all curated and filtered through the lens of corporate interests. Beneath the surface, however, these choices are far from free; they are preordained, the result of billions spent on market research, psychological profiling, and advertising campaigns designed to direct purchasing decisions in very specific ways.

In politics, the illusion of choice manifests through the facade of democratic elections. Voters are presented with a choice between candidates, each promising to act in the public's best interest, yet both often beholden to the same corporate interests. The political system, far from being a forum for the expression of the will of the people, is instead a battleground where the wealthy and powerful can engage in a war of ideas designed to keep the status quo intact. The candidates are not chosen on the basis of their commitment to public welfare, but by the extent to which they are able to garner the financial support necessary to fund their campaigns. The outcome of elections is thus predetermined not by the democratic process, but by the financial machinery that underpins it.

Even within the supposed realm of personal liberty, the choices available to individuals are constrained by the invisible hand of affluence. Education, healthcare, housing, and employment are the pillars of the modern individual's pursuit of happiness and self-determination. Yet these pillars are increasingly controlled by the wealthy, whose ability to shape the markets and institutions that govern these areas renders many of the choices we perceive to be ours, meaningless. Access to quality education, for instance, is increasingly determined by wealth rather than merit, with the best institutions becoming the preserve of the affluent, while the rest are relegated to subpar alternatives. In healthcare, individuals are forced to navigate a complex, profit-driven system where the right to good care is often dependent not on need, but on financial capability.

Housing markets, similarly, operate under the influence of financial elites who have commodified living space to such an extent that what should be a basic human right has become a luxury reserved for the rich. The rhetoric of homeownership as the cornerstone of the American Dream has been hollowed out, replaced by an environment where housing is treated not as a necessity, but as a speculative investment driven by the interests of developers, real estate moguls, and financial institutions. The individual's right to a home is no longer a given; it is a choice, yes, but one limited to those who can afford it.

Even in the realm of employment, the notion of personal choice is increasingly circumscribed by the dominance of multinational corporations and the growing power of a small corporate elite. Workers may have the "choice" of where to work, but in many industries, this choice is dictated by the structural forces that define the labor market. The commodification of work, the rise of gig economies, and the consolidation of power in a few multinational giants have stripped away many of the freedoms once associated with labor. The worker, once able to negotiate terms of employment, now faces an economy where wages are suppressed, benefits are minimal, and the stability of a career is increasingly rare.

The most insidious aspect of this engineered freedom is its self-perpetuating nature. The illusion of choice is so deeply ingrained in the collective consciousness that the very idea of constraint is obscured. The masses, bombarded by endless options, are lulled into a false sense of agency, convinced that their decisions matter, when in fact, their choices are limited and shaped by the very forces that claim to empower them. This sense of autonomy is the ultimate triumph of the powerful—the ability to convince those who are subjugated that they are free, even as their options are circumscribed by the economic and political systems that privilege the rich.

This manufactured freedom is further reinforced by the ideological underpinnings of neoliberalism, which asserts that individual success is a direct result of personal effort and ingenuity. This narrative serves to justify inequality, as it frames the wealth gap not as a product of systemic exploitation, but as the natural outcome of individual choice. If one succeeds, it is because they made the "right" choices; if one fails, it is because they did not. The myth of meritocracy, in its most insidious form, blames the individual for their lack of success, while excusing the structural barriers that perpetuate inequality.

Ultimately, the illusion of choice is not merely a tool of consumerism, politics, or labor it is the mechanism by which the powerful maintain control over the lives of the many. By presenting a world in which individuals believe they have the freedom to choose, the wealthy ensure that their dominance remains unchallenged. Freedom, in this sense, is not the absence of constraint but the very tool by which those constraints are imposed. It is not the power to choose that defines liberty; it is the recognition that, within the boundaries set by wealth and power, all choices are, in fact, illusions.

Six

The Masters of Puppets: The Global Reach of Wealth and Power

In the intricate latticework of global power, the most potent forces are often invisible, operating from behind the scenes, shaping the destinies of nations and individuals without ever appearing on the public stage. The modern world, draped in the fabric of choice, democracy, and freedom, hides a far darker reality one in which wealth does not merely sit at the helm of society, but wields an unseen, pervasive control over nearly every aspect of life. The true wielders of global influence are not those who govern openly, but those who, from the shadows, pull the strings of politics, economics, and culture. These are the masters of puppets, whose power reaches far beyond the borders of any single nation, whose influence extends to the farthest corners of the earth.

In the past, the seat of power was often tied to military might or territorial expansion, and while these methods of control are still in play in some forms, the real engines of modern dominance lie in the hands of the few who control wealth. Power in the twenty-first century is not simply concentrated in national capitals or political institutions but is instead dispersed through the global mechanisms of finance and economics, where vast fortunes dictate the terms of engagement, from trade agreements to resource allocation, and from the decisions made in the halls of government to the very structures of everyday life.

Wealth has become the invisible hand that shapes the world in ways that few truly understand. Through the quiet consolidation of financial power, a small group of individuals and entities have managed to craft an environment in which their interests are secured at all costs. The creation of this new order has been achieved not through military conquest, but through the steady and relentless accumulation of capital, which allows its holders to bend the forces of the economy and politics to their will. This concentration of wealth and power allows these elites to dominate every major arena of society be it in shaping the direction of public policy, controlling the flow of resources, or even steering the very narratives that define how society views itself.

These masters of wealth operate without allegiance to any one nation, and their influence transcends borders. They do not function within the parameters of traditional governance but instead inhabit the shadowy spaces between states, where their influence goes largely unchallenged. Nations, once seen as the paramount entities of power, are increasingly powerless in the face of the economic forces controlled by this elite. Public policy is often driven not by the will of the people, but by the unseen pressures exerted by those who control the flow of capital. Governments, regardless of their political stripes, are forced to navigate the delicate balance between the demands of their citizens and the overwhelming influence of those who pull the strings from behind closed doors.

This influence operates through a myriad of mechanisms strategic financial investments, control over resources, and the creation of complex webs of interdependency that entrap both individuals and entire economies. The puppetmasters do not need to act with overt force; instead, they manipulate from afar, ensuring that their wealth flows freely across borders and markets, fueling industries and dictating the global distribution of power. The choices available to individuals, whether in the marketplace or in political participation, are often not choices at all, but preordained outcomes carefully constructed through a lattice of financial interests, private dealings, and unseen alliances.

One of the most insidious aspects of this power is its ability to disguise itself. Wealth does not need to rely on coercion or direct domination; it creates a system in which those with capital have access to all the levers of influence. Through the manipulation of economic conditions and the careful construction of policies that favor their continued prosperity, the puppetmasters ensure that their interests remain entrenched. The public, lulled into a sense of participation, continues to believe in the myth of democracy and free markets, unaware that the true power resides not in their hands, but in those who control the essential components of society money, resources, and influence.

In politics, the illusion of democratic choice is maintained through the appearance of open debate, competition, and participation. But in reality, the political landscape is shaped by those with the financial means to back candidates and causes that align with their interests. The machinery of government has been so thoroughly intertwined with the forces of wealth that political leaders elected to represent the people often find themselves beholden to the very economic powers that funded their rise. In this new world order, the distinction between the public interest and the private interests of the wealthy elite becomes increasingly difficult to discern. Policies are framed not to address the needs of the populace, but to ensure the continued dominance of those who hold the purse strings.

The media, too, serves as a vital instrument in the hands of these puppetmasters. The narratives that shape public perception are carefully constructed to preserve the status quo and ensure that the public remains passive in the face of structural injustice. Through selective framing, omission of critical information, and the perpetuation of superficial conflicts, the media maintains an environment in which the real drivers of inequality remain obscured. The people are fed a steady diet of distractions, half-truths, and sensationalism, ensuring that the deep-seated power dynamics remain invisible to all but those who are truly paying attention.

But for all their power, the puppetmasters are not without their vulnerabilities. The global system they have crafted is precarious, dependent on the continuation of a deeply unequal structure that benefits the few at the expense of the many. As inequality grows, and as the demands for justice and equity become more pronounced, the elite must increasingly rely on the tools of coercion and control to maintain their grip on power. The rise of surveillance, the erosion of civil liberties, and the militarization of law enforcement in various parts of the world signal that the puppetmasters are aware of the growing unrest that threatens their carefully constructed order.

Yet even as they seek to tighten their hold, the cracks in the system become more apparent. Revolutions, whether in the form of mass protests, social movements, or geopolitical shifts, arise from the disillusionment of those who have been kept in the dark, those who recognize the illusion for what it is. The masses, long manipulated into believing they are powerless, are awakening to the reality of their own agency. Should the very system of control collapse or should the anger of the disenfranchised reach a tipping point the puppeteers might find themselves unseated, their strings cut by those they have long sought to control.

In the end, the puppetmasters are bound to the system they have created, and the very threads of power they pull are woven into a structure that could, at any moment, unravel. The irony of their position lies in this fundamental truth: the more they attempt to control, the more they expose their own fragility. Behind every string pulled, behind every financial transaction designed to manipulate the course of history, is a system built on instability, a house of cards poised to fall.

The masters of the modern world may rule with the ease of those who understand the intricacies of power, but they do so with the knowledge that their reign is built on a delicate balance. In a world of shadows, where the most powerful actors remain unseen, the game is never as simple as it appears. In the end, the true power lies not in the hands of the puppeteers, but in those they attempt to control who may, one day, decide to cut the strings.

Seven

The Architecture of Illusion: How Wealth Designs Perception and Reality

In the labyrinth of modern life, where the boundaries between truth and fiction blur with increasing ease, one thing remains unassailable: the power to shape perception is, without question, the most effective tool in the arsenal of the wealthy elite. What we perceive as reality our beliefs, our values, the very structure of society is not an organic product of collective human experience, but a meticulously crafted illusion, sculpted with precision by those who wield the most powerful currency: wealth. Like master architects, the wealthy design and curate the very framework through which we interpret the world, subtly guiding our thoughts, desires, and actions toward their own ends.

At the heart of this architecture of illusion lies the understanding that perception is not merely a passive reflection of external truths, but a construct shaped by external forces. The most profound forces that shape our understanding of reality are not physical, but psychological, rooted in the narratives we are fed, the images we consume, and the values that are instilled in us from a young age. The puppeteers of this grand illusion understand that the most effective form of control is not brute force, but the ability to control how reality is framed and understood. They do not need to coerce; they simply need to direct our attention and shape the way we view the world around us.

The media is the primary medium through which this manipulation unfolds. News, entertainment, and advertising become the scaffolding upon which the architecture of illusion is built. Through a carefully constructed narrative, these powerful forces curate a version of reality that serves their interests one that promotes consumption, perpetuates inequality, and distracts from the systemic forces of oppression and exploitation. Stories are told, not to inform, but to reinforce the status quo, to create the illusion of fairness and meritocracy, and to divert attention from the underlying inequalities that permeate every aspect of life.

In the realm of politics, the architecture of illusion is even more subtle. Leaders are not chosen based on their true abilities to represent the interests of the people, but according to their alignment with the economic powers that pull the strings behind the scenes. Campaigns are not won with ideas, but with image carefully crafted personas, media narratives, and strategically staged events. The electorate, seemingly in control of their own fate, is instead subjected to a continuous cycle of manipulation, designed to ensure that their choices are constrained within the parameters set by those who control the financial and political machinery of society. Democracy becomes a facade, not because the institutions themselves are flawed, but because the very process is a carefully orchestrated performance, with outcomes dictated in advance by the distribution of wealth and power.

Yet this illusion is not confined solely to the political or media sphere. Wealth, in its most insidious form, shapes our very understanding of success, achievement, and self-worth. The notion of individual merit, the idea that anyone can succeed if they work hard enough, is perhaps the most potent lie of all. It serves to justify the deeply entrenched inequalities that exist within society, offering a false narrative that those who are wealthy deserve their position, while those who struggle are simply the victims of their own inadequacy. The wealthy perpetuate this myth, not because they believe it to be true, but because it serves their interests. It keeps the masses striving for an unattainable ideal, while ensuring that the systems of power remain intact, untouched, and perpetually unchallenged.

This illusion extends to the realm of technology and consumerism. In a world where technology has become both a tool of liberation and a mechanism of control, the architecture of illusion is most visible. The digital age has ushered in an era of unprecedented connectivity and access to information. Yet, it is this very access that is used to create a fragmented, disorienting reality, in which people are constantly bombarded with data, advertisements, and curated content designed to distract and sedate. The vast web of information that seems to offer boundless opportunities for personal growth and empowerment is, in reality, a carefully controlled landscape, where the wealthiest corporations and individuals dictate the terms of engagement.

The very devices we hold in our hands, which promise to connect us to the world, are in fact the conduits through which we are subjected to an endless flow of influence, manipulation, and commodification. Social media, once heralded as the democratizing force of the digital revolution, is in many ways the most powerful mechanism in the architecture of illusion. It is not a platform for free expression, but a carefully curated environment in which individual desires, opinions, and identities are monetized and sold to the highest bidder. The algorithms that govern our interactions are not designed to serve the public good, but to ensure that our attention is captured, our data harvested, and our consumer behavior influenced in ways that benefit those who control the platform.

The world of luxury and branding, too, plays a crucial role in perpetuating the illusion. The symbols of wealth be it a designer label, an expensive car, or an exclusive vacation serve not only as markers of social status, but as tools of psychological manipulation. They create a false sense of aspiration, a desire for things that are not only unattainable for the vast majority, but are, in many ways, unnecessary and hollow. Yet, through the power of branding, these symbols are elevated to the status of cultural ideals, representing success, fulfillment, and happiness. The wealthy use this imagery to reinforce their position, creating an artificial hierarchy in which those who consume are made to believe that their worth is tied to what they own, not who they are.

The architecture of illusion is not simply a passive system of control, but an active and ever-evolving process. Those who wield power understand that in order to maintain their dominance, they must continually adapt their strategies, stay ahead of shifting societal currents, and refine their ability to manipulate perception. They are not merely reactionary actors; they are the designers of a reality that serves their interests. Through their understanding of human psychology, their mastery of media and messaging, and their unparalleled access to financial resources, they are able to craft a world in which their power remains invisible, unquestioned, and ever-expanding.

Yet, as with all illusions, the reality beneath the surface is far more fragile than it appears. The more elaborate the architecture, the more precarious the illusion becomes. The more power that is concentrated in the hands of the few, the more tenuous their grip on control. As people begin to wake up to the nature of this illusion understanding that their desires, their choices, and their realities have been shaped by forces beyond their control the architecture begins to crumble. The illusion may hold for a time, but the cracks will inevitably appear. And when they do, the structure of power that has so carefully been constructed will be revealed for what it is: a house of cards, waiting to fall.

Eight

The Empire of Consumption: How Desire Is Engineered

In the modern world, desire is not a natural force; it is a crafted artifact, a product of an intricate machinery designed to shape and channel our every yearning. What we believe to be our own desires the longings that propel us toward certain objects, lifestyles, or ideals are, in fact, meticulously constructed by those who hold the reins of wealth and power. The empire of consumption, with its sprawling networks of media, advertising, and strategic branding, works tirelessly to manufacture the very essence of human longing, transforming instinctive urges into compulsive, artificial appetites that can only be satisfied by purchasing more, consuming more, and ultimately becoming more entangled in the ever-expanding web of capitalistic desire.

At the core of this empire lies an understanding of human psychology so profound that it borders on the manipulative. The architects of consumption know that desire is not merely an impulse; it is a malleable construct, susceptible to influence and modification. By tapping into the deepest recesses of the human psyche, they have learned how to awaken latent needs needs that people themselves may not even recognize as desires transforming them into urgent, insatiable cravings. In the world of consumerism, nothing is left to chance. Every image, every slogan, every product is carefully designed to evoke a specific emotional response, creating an invisible but powerful bond between the consumer and the commodity.

This manufactured desire is not confined to any particular class or social strata; it permeates all levels of society, reinforcing an artificial hierarchy of needs. The wealthy, who understand the power of consumption better than anyone, become both the architects and the beneficiaries of this system. They design the products that people are led to covet, not merely for their functionality, but for the symbolic status they represent. The consumption of luxury goods, cutting-edge technology, and branded experiences is not simply about acquiring material possessions; it is about acquiring social currency, an emblem of belonging to an exclusive world, a world where true power resides.

Through the alchemy of branding, companies have learned to infuse their products with meanings far beyond their intrinsic value. The simplest of objects be it a car, a watch, or a bottle of perfume becomes imbued with narratives of prestige, success, and aspiration. The brand itself evolves from a mere label to a powerful symbol, one that defines identity and positions the consumer within a larger societal narrative. The act of consumption is transformed from a basic exchange of goods to a performative ritual, a statement of who one is, who one aspires to be, and where one stands in the broader social order.

The architects of this empire know that to sustain the momentum of consumption, desire must be continually stoked and reinvigorated. The fleeting satisfaction that comes from acquiring a coveted object is never enough; it is but a momentary reprieve in an endless cycle of craving. The key to perpetuating this cycle is the constant creation of new desires, the invention of new products and experiences that promise fulfillment but inevitably fail to deliver. This perpetual discontent the belief that happiness lies just beyond reach, in the next purchase or the next trend ensures that consumers remain locked in a state of perpetual desire, constantly chasing after the illusion of satisfaction.

The empire of consumption also thrives on the illusion of choice. In reality, the so-called freedom to choose from an array of products is an artifice, a sleight of hand designed to mask the underlying uniformity of the options available. Consumers are presented with a range of choices, but all of these choices are, in essence, variations on the same underlying theme: the need to consume. Whether it is a new smartphone model, a luxury handbag, or a vacation to an exotic destination, the underlying message remains the same: consume, buy, acquire, and in doing so, you will find your place in the world. The illusion of choice is a mere diversion, a strategy to keep consumers pacified as they race toward an ever-moving finish line, never realizing that the race itself is the trap.

Even more insidious is the subtle erosion of personal identity in the face of consumption. The more people buy into the idea that they can define themselves through what they own, the less they come to understand themselves beyond the confines of the marketplace. Identity becomes commodified, a product that can be shaped, molded, and sold like any other good. Social media, with its curated images of aspirational lifestyles, plays a crucial role in this transformation, creating a feedback loop in which individuals are encouraged to constantly perform their identities through the things they buy and the image they project. The result is a society where self-worth is no longer derived from inner qualities or personal achievements, but from the outward display of wealth, status, and consumption.

In this empire of consumption, the very nature of freedom is subverted. The capitalist system masquerades as a promoter of individual freedom, presenting consumption as the ultimate expression of autonomy. The idea is simple: buy what you want, when you want, and you will have achieved freedom. Yet, in reality, this freedom is nothing more than a mirage, a carefully constructed illusion. The true power of consumerism lies in its ability to convince people that their desires are their own, when in fact, those desires have been carefully engineered and marketed to them. The more they consume, the more they are bound to the system, their freedoms constrained by the very choices they are led to believe they are making independently.

Furthermore, the empire of consumption has found its most effective ally in the creation of scarcity. In a world of seemingly limitless abundance, the illusion of scarcity drives demand and amplifies the value of consumer goods. Limited editions, exclusive releases, and the promise of fleeting experiences play on the human fear of missing out, compounding the need to buy now, before it is too late. This artificial scarcity not only drives up consumption but also reinforces the idea that happiness is finite, that the goods we desire are limited, and that we must act swiftly to claim our piece of the pie before others do.

However, despite the seductive power of this engineered desire, there is a growing undercurrent of resistance, an emerging awareness that the cycle of consumption is, in fact, a prison of the mind. As the gulf between the wealthy elite and the rest of society widens, as ecological and economic crises worsen, more individuals are beginning to see through the mirage. There is a dawning recognition that the endless pursuit of goods and status is not the path to fulfillment, but the very thing that stifles true freedom and joy. A new paradigm is emerging one that seeks to redefine worth, not in terms of possessions, but in terms of connection, sustainability, and authenticity.

The empire of consumption may be vast, but it is not invincible. As more people awaken to the realization that their desires have been shaped by forces beyond their control, they begin to break free from the chains of consumption. The illusion may persist for now, but the seeds of resistance are being sown, and the foundations of the empire are beginning to tremble. In the end, the desire to consume may not be the final word on human fulfillment; it may be the awakening of our deeper, more authentic desires that will lead us toward true freedom.

Nine

The Cartography of Containment: How Wealth Constructs and Dismantles Resistance

In the labyrinthine corridors of affluence, the boundaries between freedom and captivity are seldom clear. The colossal structures of capital, designed to ensure the uninterrupted flow of wealth, often obscure the very forces that perpetuate subjugation. While wealth appears as a benign force, a conduit for prosperity and progress, it quietly weaves a subtle web of containment one that both constructs and dismantles resistance with an elegance that belies its treachery. This is not a mere suppression of dissent, but a careful engineering of constraints, an architecture of control that shapes the contours of autonomy itself.

At first glance, the mechanisms of containment are difficult to decipher. They do not resemble the overt, authoritarian structures of oppressive regimes or the explicit repression of the masses. Rather, they manifest as a series of seemingly benign distractions and manipulations soft violences that keep the populace within the limits of a carefully curated, narrow freedom. The illusion of choice becomes the first and most insidious tool in the arsenal of containment. The very notion that individuals possess agency is often the trap itself. These choices, though presented as varied and abundant, exist within a constrained framework, designed not to empower but to neutralize potential for true rebellion. The freedom of selection is not the freedom to escape, but the freedom to reinforce the status quo.

Wealth, in this context, does not merely serve as a force of attraction but as a tool of confinement. The allure of consumption is one of its most effective strategies. Consumerism, as it exists in the gilded halls of affluence, is less about desire and more about pacification. The act of acquiring the endless pursuit of the new, the novel, the fashionable functions as a subtle form of pacification, turning discontent into distraction. By promoting an ever-expanding cycle of desire, wealth creates an environment in which resistance is rendered redundant. When dissatisfaction emerges, it is swiftly subsumed into the economy of consumption. Rebellion is not crushed outright but absorbed, repackaged, and sold back as a commodity.

Yet, even within this systematic containment, pockets of resistance however small or fragmented continue to appear. These resistances are not always overt; they do not always take the form of organized protests or explicit defiance. Instead, they manifest as moments of dissonance, as fractures in the seamless narrative that wealth seeks to construct. Such fractures, though often invisible to the naked eye, are nonetheless critical in understanding the complex dynamics of control. They are the outliers, the voices on the periphery that refuse to be fully absorbed by the machine.

The response to these fractures is equally sophisticated. Resistance, rather than being eradicated, is redirected and neutralized through a process of co-optation. The very elements of dissent that threaten to disrupt the system are, through subtle means, integrated into the larger structure of affluence. What was once a spark of rebellion is transformed into an acceptable form of dissent one that does not jeopardize the flow of capital. Movements, ideologies, and critiques that could challenge the system are often embraced, commodified, and marketed back to the public in a palatable form. The result is a paradox: resistance is allowed to exist, but it exists on the condition that it does not truly disrupt the flow of wealth and power.

In this grand scheme of containment, the architecture of resistance is itself engineered. The very design of opposition is shaped by the forces it seeks to challenge. What begins as an attempt to break free from the chains of wealth and power is often reduced to another cog in the machine another marketable product, another aspect of the culture industry. In this way, wealth ensures its dominance not through the overt destruction of its critics, but through the absorption and transformation of those critics into its own narrative.

This manipulation extends beyond the realm of consumption into the domain of information. The narratives that shape our understanding of power are themselves carefully constructed, filtered through a lens that preserves the status quo. The flow of knowledge is controlled, shaped by the interests of those who wield wealth. What is deemed acceptable knowledge becomes a reflection of what supports the continuation of the established order, while alternative perspectives are marginalized or erased. The control of information, then, is not only about maintaining power, but about ensuring that the very foundations of resistance are obscured, their potential nullified before they can gain traction.

But perhaps the most subtle and dangerous form of containment is the manipulation of time itself. The pace of contemporary life speeding ever faster in the pursuit of profit and expansion creates a temporal dissonance that prevents meaningful reflection and critical thought. The continuous churn of activity, the relentless pursuit of productivity, leaves little room for the kind of introspection or collective deliberation that might challenge the established order. Time, as it is structured by wealth, becomes a form of control, a tool that keeps the populace perpetually occupied, always moving forward but never truly progressing.

In this context, the very concept of freedom becomes mutable, fluid. What does it mean to be free when all paths are hedged, all choices are circumscribed by the larger system of wealth and power? How can one resist when every attempt at resistance is co-opted, redirected, or consumed? The struggle against containment, in the age of affluence, is not just about breaking free from physical constraints, but about shattering the illusion of choice itself.

This is the paradox of wealth and power: it does not merely dominate through force, but through the creation of an environment in which the very notion of resistance becomes impossible to sustain. To break free from this architecture of containment requires more than just rejecting the external manifestations of power; it requires the dismantling of the underlying assumptions upon which the entire system is built.

The true task of resistance, then, lies not in overthrowing a single institution or regime, but in unraveling the complex, multi-layered web that sustains the system of affluence. It is a task that requires both vision and tenacity, an understanding that the boundaries of power are not just imposed externally, but embedded in the very structure of our daily lives.

And so, as the boat of affluence sails ever forward, one must ask: can we navigate the waters of wealth and control, or are we doomed to sail upside down, forever adrift in a sea of illusion?

Ten

The Specter of Erosion: How Wealth Corrodes the Fabric of Justice

The pervasive hand of wealth does not merely control the tangible apparatus of power; it subtly erodes the very principles upon which justice is constructed. Far from a solitary or obvious force, this corrosion operates insidiously, creeping into the recesses of legal, social, and ethical frameworks. It chips away at the bedrock of fairness, transforming justice from a once-pristine ideal into a malleable commodity, shaped by the whims of those with the means to manipulate it. In this new paradigm, justice is not blind, as the myth would have it, but myopic focused narrowly on the interests of the wealthy, while the larger society languishes in the shadow of its indifference.

The erosion of justice begins with the commodification of legality itself. Law, once considered a neutral arbiter of rights and wrongs, has increasingly come to resemble a marketplace where the highest bidder receives favorable treatment. What was once the safeguard of the vulnerable has now become a tool of those who can afford to bend it to their will. The costs of legal battles often astronomical in their scope exclude all but the most affluent from seeking genuine redress. The consequences of this are manifold, for in a system where legal protection is not a universal right but a commodity, the powerful are free to transgress, while the powerless are consigned to the margins of justice, unable to fight back.

This distortion of law is compounded by the notion of "legal agility," a euphemism for the ability to exploit loopholes, manipulate statutes, and engage in lengthy legal battles that drain resources and exhaust opposition. Such tactics, while often technically legal, are corrosive to the spirit of justice. They create a system where outcomes are determined not by the merits of a case, but by the depth of one's pockets and the dexterity of one's legal team. In such a system, law becomes a game, played at the highest stakes, with those on the lower rungs of society relegated to mere spectators, powerless in the face of a game they cannot afford to enter.

At its core, justice is meant to reflect a balance an equilibrium between rights and responsibilities, protections and freedoms. When wealth enters the equation, however, this balance tilts, slowly at first, then precipitously, towards inequality. The forces of capital exacerbate disparities by entwining themselves with the institutions meant to uphold fairness, creating a situation where power and privilege perpetuate themselves, not through merit, but through control over the mechanisms of justice. This control manifests in myriad ways: the funding of political campaigns that shape judicial appointments; the subjugation of prosecutorial offices to corporate interests; the infiltration of lobbying groups into the very heart of legislative and judicial processes. These are not accidents of governance, but deliberate efforts to align the machinery of justice with the economic and political interests of the wealthy few.

This systemic capture of justice is not merely a matter of individual corruption, though such instances are commonplace. Rather, it is a structural flaw built into the architecture of affluence itself. The very design of wealth and power necessitates this distortion, for it is only through the manipulation of legal structures that the flow of capital can remain uninterrupted and unchallenged. The wealthy do not simply wield power; they engineer the very frameworks within which power operates. Legal institutions, once entrusted with safeguarding the public good, are gradually repurposed to serve the private interests of the few, their original mandate of equity rendered hollow by the corrosive influence of money.

The result of this erosion is a society in which justice is no longer a shared experience but a fractured and fragmented ideal. Justice is no longer an egalitarian force; it is a variable, shaped by the wealth of the individual. The consequences of this shift are profound. When justice becomes the province of the affluent, the very concept of fairness becomes elusive. Those who are caught in the webs of inequality whether through systemic racism, economic exploitation, or corporate malfeasance find themselves locked out of the legal system, their pleas unheard, their grievances dismissed as inconsequential. Meanwhile, those with the resources to manipulate the system exploit its loopholes, twisting the law to suit their ends, ensuring that they remain free from accountability.

Yet, even within this landscape of corrosion, the illusion of justice persists. It is a spectral apparition, haunting the corridors of power, perpetuated by rhetoric and symbolism but hollowed out in practice. The courts remain open, the judges remain seated, and the laws remain written. But beneath the surface, the very essence of justice has been hollowed out, turned into a form of ceremonial theatre an elaborate spectacle that distracts the public from the realities of legal manipulation and economic exploitation. The appearance of justice becomes a tool of control, as those in power maintain the myth of fairness while systematically stripping away its substance.

It is in this theatre of justice that the true nature of wealth's malfeasance is most vividly revealed. For the wealthy, justice is not a fundamental principle but a tool one to be bent, shaped, and used to reinforce their dominance. In this light, wealth does not just corrupt justice; it redefines it, transforms it from a concept of equality and fairness into a system of privileges and exemptions. The machinery of law becomes nothing more than a façade, a mask behind which the powerful operate with impunity, shielded from the consequences of their actions by the very structures designed to protect the common good.

But there is, perhaps, an even deeper irony in this corrosion: the more wealth intertwines itself with justice, the more justice becomes a distant abstraction, its practical meaning eroded to the point of irrelevance. In a society where law is contingent upon wealth, the very foundations of civic trust crumble. The belief that justice can be achieved through legal means falters, and with it, the legitimacy of the entire system. People begin to question not only the fairness of the law but the very concept of law itself. What is justice, after all, if it is available only to those with the means to acquire it?

Thus, the erosion of justice is not just an issue of the disenfranchised; it is a crisis of legitimacy, one that undermines the moral and ethical foundations of society as a whole. When justice becomes a commodity something to be bought and sold its core value vanishes, and with it, the trust that binds a society together.

In this age of wealth and affluence, the challenge is not simply to reform the legal system, but to confront the underlying structures of power that enable such corruption to thrive. It is only by dismantling the systems that perpetuate economic inequality, that enshroud justice in a veil of commodification, that the true meaning of fairness can be reclaimed. Until then, justice will remain little more than a ghost an ideal once noble, now hollowed out by the corrosive power of wealth.

Eleven

The Alchemy of Illusion:
Transforming Moral Decay into Virtue

In the rarefied air where wealth and power converge, the manipulation of perception becomes not merely an art but an alchemical process. Here, moral decay is transmuted into virtue, vice into benevolence, and exploitation into philanthropy. The methods employed to achieve this inversion are as old as power itself, yet their mastery has reached unprecedented heights in the modern age. What was once seen as greed, self-interest, or indifference is rebranded as generosity, innovation, and civic duty. This is the great illusion, the sleight of hand that allows the architects of affluence to maintain their stranglehold on society while projecting an image of righteousness and benevolence. It is a masterclass in the manipulation of morality, a careful orchestration that ensures the wealthiest remain untouchable, their moral transgressions obscured by the fog of their manufactured virtue.

The process begins with what might be called the aestheticization of power. Power, in its most naked and unapologetic form, is often an ugly thing: it is coercive, self-serving, and frequently destructive. Yet, in the hands of those who wield vast wealth, this ugliness is carefully concealed beneath a veneer of nobility. The transformation is subtle but profound. A person who has amassed wealth not through industriousness but by exploiting systemic imbalances, who has used influence to shape policies that benefit only a select few, is reframed as a "visionary" or "philanthropist." Their actions, no matter how self-interested, are reinterpreted as contributions to the common good. This rebranding is not accidental. It is the result of a carefully crafted narrative, one that rewrites the terms of the conversation about power and virtue.

A key tool in this alchemical process is the celebration of the self-made individual. The myth of the self-made billionaire, the entrepreneur who rose from nothing to claim his fortune, has become a central trope in the narrative of modern affluence. This myth is deeply appealing, for it promises that anyone, regardless of background, can achieve greatness through determination and innovation. It evokes images of meritocracy and individual agency. But this myth is itself a crucial element of the illusion. For while the wealthy are celebrated for their supposed autonomy and rugged individualism, the structural advantages that sustain their wealth are quietly obscured. In reality, many of the self-made fortunes were built on the backs of hidden labor, systemic injustices, and economic privileges that remain invisible to the broader public. To present wealth as the product of personal merit alone is to engage in an act of historical amnesia, erasing the factors that allow certain individuals to rise while others are systematically crushed.

Once this veneer of self-sufficiency is established, it can be extended into the realm of social responsibility. The wealthy, having consolidated their power, are increasingly presented not as the benefactors of their own success, but as the architects of social good. The "philanthropist" emerges as a central figure in this narrative: a billionaire who donates vast sums of money to charitable causes, funds groundbreaking medical research, or builds educational institutions that promise to uplift the disenfranchised. These charitable acts are framed as evidence of moral rectitude, the outward signs of a benevolent spirit. And yet, behind the philanthropy lies a cold, calculating logic: charity becomes a mechanism of self-preservation, a means to whitewash one's public image and stave off scrutiny.

In truth, philanthropy often serves a dual purpose. On one hand, it provides the illusion of virtue, reinforcing the notion that wealth, in its purest form, is a force for good. On the other, it perpetuates the very structures that necessitate charity in the first place. The wealthy are not interested in dismantling the systems that enable their accumulation of power and resources; they are interested in preserving those systems, while deflecting moral criticism through acts of superficial generosity. This dynamic is the crux of the moral paradox of affluence: by becoming the arbiters of charity, the wealthy present themselves as moral stewards of society, while maintaining the economic structures that sustain inequality. In essence, they are both the architects of the problem and the solution a paradox that obscures the deeper, structural forces at play.

Philanthropy, thus, becomes a tool of moral laundering. It is the act of cleaning one's conscience by performing acts that appear virtuous on the surface but ultimately preserve the status quo. The wealthy, rather than addressing the systemic inequities that allow their fortunes to flourish, engage in a kind of moral accounting, where their donations, no matter how large, serve as a kind of offset for their participation in the structural injustices that generate their wealth. The public, in turn, is invited to accept this narrative, to see the donation as the end of the conversation, rather than the beginning of a deeper critique.

But this alchemy does not end with philanthropy. It extends into the realm of culture creation, where wealth is used to shape not only policy and economics, but ideas and values. Through media, art, and entertainment, the rich craft a narrative that portrays their accumulation of wealth as a natural, even virtuous outcome of innovation and hard work. They fund museums, sponsor films, and support high-profile cultural events, all of which perpetuate the image of the wealthy as not just powerful, but cultured and refined. In doing so, they entrench the idea that wealth is synonymous with merit and wisdom, that those who have succeeded in amassing fortune are, by extension, the guardians of culture and civilization itself. The cultural elite, then, are elevated as the stewards of good taste and moral propriety, and their opinions on matters of public policy and social justice are imbued with an unwarranted authority.

This manipulation of culture extends to the manufacture of consent. The wealthiest individuals, through their control of media and information networks, are able to shape the very narratives that define public discourse. What is considered "right" or "wrong," "ethical" or "immoral," is not determined by the collective will of the people, but by those who control the flow of information. In this way, wealth shapes not just the physical structures of power, but the very consciousness of society. Public opinion becomes a tool to be molded and directed, rather than an organic reflection of the people's needs and desires.

In this grand alchemical process, the line between truth and illusion blurs. Power, once naked and unadorned, is transformed into something pure, noble, and virtuous. Greed becomes a form of enlightened self-interest, exploitation becomes innovation, and inequality becomes a byproduct of progress. This is the triumph of perception over reality, the victory of illusion over substance. The wealthy, by controlling not only the means of production but the means of perception, create a world in which their dominance is not only unchallenged but celebrated as a moral good.

The true cost of this transformation is the erosion of critical consciousness. When the illusion is sufficiently polished, when virtue is so seamlessly interwoven with wealth and power, the very idea of questioning it becomes almost unthinkable. The alchemy of illusion is so convincing that even those who are most directly harmed by the existing system are often lulled into a passive acceptance of their place within it. The machinery of exploitation continues, but its true nature remains obscured by the fog of moral misdirection.

The greatest trick of affluence is not simply the amassing of wealth, but the transformation of that wealth into a force for righteousness, in the eyes of both the public and the wielders of power themselves. The wealthy do not just control the resources of the world; they control its values, its narratives, and its understanding of what is just and virtuous.

as analysis, this alchemical manipulation is the true measure of the wealth's power: the ability to turn vice into virtue, decay into prosperity, and exploitation into philanthropy, while maintaining an iron grip on both the material and moral foundations of society.

Twelve

The Mirage of Stability: How Wealth Manufactures the Illusion of Order

In the vast, turbulent seas of political and economic systems, the appearance of stability is often more fragile than it seems. Yet, for those who control the currents of wealth, stability is not merely a product of chance or necessity it is a carefully curated illusion. Beneath the veneer of calm and order, the true mechanics of affluence are driven by relentless forces of exploitation, manipulation, and control. The architects of wealth do not merely accumulate capital; they fabricate a facade of stability, a semblance of peace and predictability, in order to safeguard their interests and perpetuate the myth of a just and functioning society. This mirage, expertly constructed and maintained, ensures that the masses remain placid, sedated by the illusion of a stable world, while the architects of this stability continue to steer the ship of affluence in their own direction.

The first element in this illusion is the manufacture of consensus. In a world marked by stark inequalities and entrenched power structures, the idea that social and political order exists because it reflects the collective will of the people is, at best, a convenient fiction. The wealthy do not rely on the spontaneity of popular will to maintain order; they create it through the strategic deployment of ideology, narrative, and spectacle. What is presented to the public as a natural and inevitable social contract is, in reality, a carefully constructed edifice designed to reinforce existing power relations.

The architects of affluence do not allow society to drift into chaos, for chaos threatens their control. Instead, they engineer a sense of unity an illusion of harmony between classes, races, and nations. This unity is fostered not through genuine reconciliation, but through the careful propagation of ideals that serve to pacify the discontented and maintain the status quo. The media, political institutions, and cultural narratives are all co-opted into the service of this grand design. Through the manipulation of information, the wealthy ensure that the appearance of social cohesion is maintained, even as the underlying forces of inequality, exploitation, and environmental destruction intensify.

The second pillar of this constructed stability is the management of dissent. In a society where the mechanisms of wealth and power are so starkly uneven, resistance is inevitable. Yet, the wealthy do not seek to stamp out opposition entirely. Instead, they adopt a more insidious strategy: they contain, redirect, and ultimately neutralize dissent. Protests, uprisings, and calls for reform are not quelled by outright repression alone, but by creating controlled outlets through which frustration can be expressed without disrupting the larger system.

This is where the politics of tolerance come into play. The wealthy, as the creators of this illusionary order, often embrace a rhetoric of inclusivity, diversity, and progressive change. They fund social movements, sponsor grassroots organizations, and even engage in symbolic gestures of solidarity with marginalized communities. However, these gestures are never truly transformative. The wealthy, by controlling the means of both production and protest, ensure that any challenge to the system remains within predefined boundaries. Dissent is no longer a direct threat to the power structure; it is commodified, packaged, and then sold back to the public as a form of acceptable, "safe" resistance.

Thus, even the most vociferous protests or revolutionary movements become a part of the larger spectacle of affluence. The wealthy, in their infinite resources, can afford to allow such movements to exist as long as they do not threaten the foundations of power. The language of rebellion, when carefully managed, becomes just another commodity in the marketplace of ideas one that can be consumed by the public without ever altering the systemic inequalities that underpin the status quo. In this way, dissent is co-opted and domesticated, transformed into a manageable, even marketable, force.

The third element of this manufactured order is the economy of fear a pervasive undercurrent that runs through both the political and economic systems, ensuring that stability is never truly threatened. Fear, paradoxically, is both a tool of control and a mechanism for preserving the illusion of stability. The wealthy, through the manipulation of media, finance, and political discourse, create an atmosphere of constant anxiety, whether through the specter of terrorism, the fear of economic collapse, or the existential dread of environmental catastrophe. This fear, while seemingly random or external, is in fact cultivated as a means to keep the population pliable and obedient. It serves as a reminder that stability is fragile and must be actively maintained.

In the world constructed by the wealthy, fear is not a disorderly force; it is a strategically harnessed emotion. The population is taught to fear those who seek to disrupt the established order, to fear social upheaval, to fear the unknown. This fear keeps the masses in check, reminding them that the present order, however imperfect, is preferable to the chaos of change. Fear also facilitates the continued centralization of power, as those who control the means of information and the resources of the state are seen as the only actors capable of maintaining order and protecting society from the destabilizing forces lurking in the shadows.

But the greatest illusion of all is the promise of progress. The wealthy do not merely present a static image of stability; they sell the idea that the current system is inherently progressive, that it is moving toward a better, more prosperous future for all. This vision of progress, however, is not one of equality or social justice, but of further consolidation of power. The system is portrayed as one that rewards merit, fosters innovation, and continually creates opportunities for upward mobility. But beneath this rhetoric lies a more cynical reality: the wealth generated by the system is disproportionately concentrated, and the mechanisms of power ensure that the structure remains largely unchanged.

The narrative of progress is often embodied in the figure of the innovator, the entrepreneur, or the visionary who pushes the boundaries of technology, science, or industry. These figures are celebrated not only for their economic success but for their ability to "transform the world," to create new possibilities. However, the promise of progress, like all other illusions, serves only to mask the true nature of wealth's accumulation. Progress is framed as inevitable, a force that moves society forward, yet the very structures that maintain wealth and power are entrenched, even as the veneer of progress is polished. The illusion is simple: if the system is constantly moving forward, then its inherent injustices are either irrelevant or self-correcting.

This manufactured illusion of progress is reinforced by the myth of the neutral market. In the world of affluence, the market is often presented as a neutral arbiter of value, a force that rewards hard work and innovation while punishing inefficiency and stagnation. In this myth, the market is not an arena shaped by power, but a fair and impartial judge of success and failure. Yet, the very nature of the market, in a system where wealth is concentrated and opportunities are limited, ensures that those at the top remain there, while the rest of society remains tethered to the bottom. The myth of a neutral market serves to obscure the ways in which wealth is not created by merit, but by the systematic extraction of value from labor, resources, and the environment.

In the final analysis, the mirage of stability is the product of a system designed not to protect the public good, but to safeguard the interests of the few. It is a fragile construction, one that relies on the manipulation of perception, the pacification of dissent, the exploitation of fear, and the distortion of progress. The true nature of stability in the world of affluence is not one of order, but of control a control that is so effective, so deeply embedded, that it often goes unnoticed. The ship of affluence sails in smooth waters, its course directed by unseen hands, while the illusion of stability lulls the masses into complacency.

Yet, beneath the placid surface, the forces of exploitation churn, ever ready to disrupt the delicate equilibrium that ensures the continued dominance of the few. The challenge, then, is not only to expose this illusion but to disrupt the very foundations upon which it is built. Until that moment arrives, the mirage will continue to shimmer on the horizon, a promise of order and progress that, like all illusions, fades the closer one approaches.

Thirteen

The Dystopia of Desire: How Wealth Engineers the Longing for Subjugation

In the modern age, affluence has transcended its traditional role as a mere accumulative force, metamorphosing into a complex system of psychological manipulation and cultural engineering. Wealth no longer simply represents the apex of material success it is the architect of human desire itself. Through subtle, pervasive mechanisms, the custodians of affluence have become the invisible masters of longing, engineering not only the consumption of goods but the consumption of identities, values, and aspirations. This is the true power of wealth: the capacity to cultivate a collective yearning for subjugation, to shape the very desires of individuals so that they willingly, even eagerly, accept their place in the hierarchical order that wealth perpetuates.

At the heart of this engineered longing lies the concept of desire as a commodity. In a world of boundless choice and apparent freedom, desire itself has been commodified, extracted from the depths of human experience, and shaped into a product to be sold back to the masses. Through advertising, media, and cultural production, the architects of affluence have learned to manipulate the deepest recesses of the human psyche, turning every wish, every impulse, into a potential market. The desires of the masses are no longer organic or autonomous but have been carefully cultivated, monitored, and harvested by those who control the systems of wealth.

This manipulation begins with the creation of artificial scarcity. Scarcity, as an economic principle, is not only a matter of physical availability but a psychological construct, one that induces a sense of urgency and longing. The more desirable something is, the more unattainable it must appear. Thus, affluence engineers desire by introducing artificial limitations on goods, services, and experiences, making them seem rare, exclusive, and thereby imbued with greater value. What the consumer does not see is that this scarcity is entirely manufactured an illusion designed to cultivate an insatiable hunger. The desire for unattainable things becomes the driving force behind consumption, while the individual, caught in the throes of yearning, becomes both the target and the tool of affluence's insidious reach.

Yet the true genius of this system lies not in the objects it creates but in the cultivation of inadequacy. To manufacture desire is not merely to create a longing for goods; it is to create a profound sense of deficiency, a feeling that one is incomplete, unfulfilled, or insufficient. Wealth exploits this vulnerability, subtly reinforcing the notion that one's worth is tied to what one possesses. The message is ubiquitous, whispered into the ears of individuals through the glow of screens, the glossy pages of magazines, and the curated images of influencers: you are not enough, but you can be, if only you acquire this thing, embody this lifestyle, embrace this identity. In this way, desire is no longer a matter of personal choice; it becomes a mechanism of self-alienation, a way for individuals to continually distance themselves from their true selves, chasing an ideal that is perpetually out of reach.

The architects of affluence do not simply offer products; they offer transformations. The consumer is not buying a car, a phone, or a vacation; they are buying the promise of becoming someone else, someone more attractive, more successful, more admired. In this world, possession is not enough. One must not only have, but must embody, the symbols of status and distinction. The distinction between need and want becomes increasingly blurred, as desires are fabricated, commodified, and reintroduced into the marketplace, so that even those who appear to have achieved fulfillment are left wanting more.

In this context, the concept of freedom undergoes a radical distortion. The promise of affluence is often cloaked in the language of personal autonomy: the ability to choose, to pursue one's desires without constraint. However, this freedom is not liberation; it is the freedom to choose within a narrow, preordained set of options. The vast array of products, services, and experiences available to the consumer may seem to offer infinite choice, but in reality, they are a tightly controlled spectrum, carefully designed to channel the individual's longings into predictable, profitable avenues. The illusion of freedom exists only insofar as the choices made do not challenge the underlying structures of power. In this context, affluence manufactures the longing for freedom itself by ensuring that the only "freedom" on offer is a freedom to be enslaved by one's desires, a freedom that perpetuates subjugation rather than liberation.

This phenomenon is most apparent in the rise of lifestyle branding the selling of identities as a form of consumption. Today, the act of purchasing is no longer merely a transaction for material goods; it is an act of self-definition. The consumer is invited to "buy into" a lifestyle, a set of values, a narrative of success and aspiration. This is not a simple transaction; it is an identity transformation, a means of shaping oneself to fit into the constructed ideals of the affluent elite. The consumer is not just buying a product; they are buying a version of themselves, one that reflects the aspirations and fantasies engineered by the purveyors of wealth.

The psychological implications of this branding are profound. In a world where identities are fluid and malleable, individuals are increasingly encouraged to think of themselves as products to be marketed, packaged, and sold. The "self" is no longer an autonomous entity but a construct, shaped and influenced by external forces. The wealthy, through the manipulation of desire, become the unseen hand guiding individuals along a path of self-exploitation. The consumer becomes both the buyer and the product, their desires packaged and sold in an endless cycle of consumption and self-reinvention.

But it is the illusion of happiness that most powerfully sustains this system of engineered desire. The promise of fulfillment is central to the narrative of affluence, and it is precisely this promise that binds individuals to the system. The wealthy understand that happiness, in the modern era, is no longer a matter of spiritual or intellectual fulfillment; it is a commodity to be purchased. Through the relentless promotion of material acquisition, they create the false belief that true happiness can be attained through the accumulation of goods and the consumption of experiences. This, of course, is an illusion. For as soon as one desire is sated, another is introduced, and the cycle of longing continues indefinitely.

This unending pursuit of happiness through consumption creates a deep sense of existential disquiet. The individual, ever chasing the next fleeting moment of gratification, remains trapped in a cycle of dissatisfaction. The wealthiest individuals, in turn, continue to profit from this insatiable desire, while the masses remain mired in the paradox of a happiness that is always just beyond their reach. This perpetual yearning becomes a mechanism of social control, for it distracts individuals from the deeper, more systemic inequalities that underpin the structure of affluence. In this way, the longing for fulfillment becomes a form of subjugation, for it keeps individuals locked in a cycle of desire that diverts their attention away from the true sources of their oppression.

What wealth achieves, then, is not just the physical subjugation of the masses through economic inequality; it is the mental and emotional subjugation of desire itself. It transforms desire from a natural expression of human need into an artificial construct an endless, consuming force that shapes individuals' lives and identities. By engineering the very desires that fuel the machinery of consumption, the architects of affluence control not only what is bought and sold but also how individuals understand themselves and their place in the world.

In the end, the dystopia of desire is one where the pursuit of happiness becomes synonymous with the pursuit of consumption, and where individuals are not only subjugated by the material conditions of their existence but by the very desires that drive them. This is the ultimate triumph of affluence: the ability to manipulate, shape, and exploit human longing itself, so that the very forces of desire work to reinforce the power structures that oppress and control.

Fourteen

The Erosion of Collective Consciousness: How History is Rewritten for Power's Sake

In a world increasingly governed by fragmented perspectives and subjective truths, the collective consciousness is slowly but inexorably eroded. What was once a shared understanding of reality the communal recognition of history, culture, and morality has been supplanted by an array of narratives, each designed to serve the interests of those in power. The architects of affluence, in their pursuit of control, recognize that the manipulation of history is one of the most potent tools in their arsenal. By rewriting the past and distorting the present, they shape the future according to their desires, obscuring the truths that might threaten their dominion.

The historical narrative, once a reflection of collective memory, is increasingly controlled by a few powerful entities governments, corporations, media conglomerates, and cultural elites. These actors not only manipulate the flow of information but actively engage in the construction of reality itself, molding the public's understanding of both past and present events. What is deemed "truth" in society is no longer based on objective facts or empirical evidence but on a carefully curated story, one that aligns with the needs and interests of those who hold power.

The first weapon in this battle for the collective mind is the reconstruction of historical memory. History, as we understand it, is not a static record of events but a narrative continually shaped and reshaped by the forces that control its telling. Those who dominate the mechanisms of communication whether through academia, media, or popular culture are the ones who determine which events are remembered and which are forgotten. What is considered "history" is not simply a chronological account of past occurrences; it is a selective, strategic recounting, designed to glorify certain figures, justify certain ideologies, and obscure the inconvenient truths that might reveal the true nature of power.

This selective memory is most evident in the way historical injustices are erased or reframed. Atrocities, whether committed by governments, corporations, or other power structures, are often minimized, sanitized, or even completely omitted from the collective memory. The atrocities of imperialism, colonialism, slavery, and exploitation fade into the background, repackaged as "necessary evils" or relegated to obscure corners of history. At the same time, the contributions of marginalized groups, those who have fought for justice, equality, and liberation, are downplayed or distorted, often reduced to footnotes in the dominant narrative. In this way, history becomes a tool not of enlightenment, but of control a mechanism that ensures that the power structures of the present are legitimized by the myths of the past.

The second aspect of this historical manipulation is the reduction of complexity. Real history is messy; it is filled with contradictions, ambiguities, and uncertainties. It is a tapestry of diverse voices, each with its own story, its own perspective. Yet, in the hands of those who control the narrative, history is flattened, simplified, and stripped of its nuance.

Complex events are distilled into easy-to-digest myths heroes versus villains, progress versus stagnation creating a false sense of clarity that serves to reinforce existing power structures. The human complexity of historical events is obscured, reduced to caricatures that serve the interests of those who wish to maintain their dominance. In this reductionist worldview, dissent becomes a form of irrationality, complexity becomes a distraction, and the truth becomes a casualty of convenience.

One of the most insidious tools in the manipulation of historical consciousness is the corporatization of culture. In the modern era, culture once a space for collective expression, dissent, and reflection has become an extension of commerce. Film, television, literature, and art, once vehicles for challenging the status quo, are now consumed as products, designed to entertain rather than enlighten. These cultural products are often produced by conglomerates with vast financial interests, whose primary aim is not the transmission of truth, but the shaping of perception. By commodifying culture, power structures ensure that the public's understanding of history, identity, and justice is shaped by narratives that uphold the status quo, narratives that reinforce the economic and political hierarchies that serve their interests.

The pervasive influence of media hegemony further distorts historical understanding. In the digital age, where information is both ubiquitous and overwhelming, the sheer volume of content drowns out the voices that might offer alternative perspectives. News outlets, social media platforms, and entertainment conglomerates many owned by a small number of corporate entities become the gatekeepers of truth. These entities not only control what information is disseminated but also dictate how that information is framed. The public is bombarded with sensationalized headlines, soundbites, and narratives that obscure the deeper, systemic forces at play in the world. In this environment, complex historical events are often reduced to simplistic dichotomies, while dissenting voices are marginalized or silenced altogether.

It is not merely the past that is distorted, however; the present too is refracted through the lens of power. In a world where surveillance capitalism reigns supreme, where every click, every purchase, every interaction is monitored and analyzed, the very notion of personal freedom and agency is undermined. In a sense, the present has been constructed not as a space for authentic experience, but as a stage for the enactment of preordained narratives, crafted by those who control the flow of information. Every story that emerges from the public sphere is shaped, framed, and manipulated to fit a particular agenda whether it be political, economic, or cultural.

This leads us to the third, and perhaps most profound, element of this historical distortion: the disempowerment of critical thought. In a world where information is constant, immediate, and often superficial, the ability to engage with history in a critical and reflective manner has been severely diminished. The sheer volume of information, coupled with the selective nature of its presentation, prevents individuals from developing a coherent understanding of the world. The public is encouraged not to think critically, but to accept the narratives handed down to them by the powers that be. The questioning of history, the exploration of its contradictions, the examination of its ethical implications these activities are sidelined in favor of passive consumption. Critical thinking becomes a niche activity, reserved for academics, intellectuals, or activists, while the majority of the population is consumed by the daily grind of survival, entertainment, and consumption.

The manipulation of historical consciousness is, in this sense, an act of social pacification. By controlling the stories we tell about ourselves and our world, the powerful ensure that the status quo remains unchallenged. The collective memory is not a living, evolving entity, but a frozen narrative one that serves the interests of those who dominate. History, once a tool of liberation and enlightenment, becomes a weapon of oppression, reinforcing the very systems that have caused suffering and injustice. The future, too, is shaped by the stories we tell about the past. If we are to break free from the grip of this historical distortion, we must first recognize that the narratives of power are not natural or inevitable; they are the product of deliberate actions, undertaken to safeguard the interests of the few.

In the final analysis, the erosion of collective consciousness is not merely a matter of forgetting it is a process of manufactured ignorance, a deliberate distortion of history to suit the needs of the powerful. To challenge this system, to reclaim the truth of our shared past, is to engage in the struggle for authentic memory, for a history that reflects the complexity and diversity of human experience. Only by confronting the lies of the past can we hope to construct a future grounded in justice, equity, and truth.

Fifteen

The Tyranny of Convenience: How Ease and Efficiency Breed Dependency

In the modern epoch, the most insidious form of oppression is not one of overt force or blatant coercion, but one of subtle convenience. The relentless march toward efficiency and comfort has engendered a form of dependency so profound that it has redefined what it means to be free. While the technological advances and innovations of the contemporary era promise liberation from the burdens of labor, they also create an inescapable web of reliance on systems that strip individuals of agency. Convenience, in its most potent form, is the opiate of the modern world, lulling societies into a stupor of passive consumption and voluntary servitude.

The concept of convenience, in the technological sense, is often heralded as the solution to human discomfort and inefficiency. It is embedded in every aspect of daily life: from the instantaneous gratification of digital communication to the omnipresent allure of consumer goods delivered to one's doorstep with the tap of a finger. Convenience, once a luxury, has become a ubiquitous necessity, an ever-present companion in the lives of individuals. The promise of ease has created a world in which everything is at hand, every desire within reach, and every need met in the shortest possible time. Yet, beneath this veneer of ease lies a deeper, more troubling reality: this convenience exacts a high cost—one that often goes unnoticed.

The first cost of convenience is the erosion of autonomy. In the pursuit of efficiency, we have relinquished the very essence of self-determination. The proliferation of digital technologies, automation, and outsourcing has rendered many tasks so effortless that individuals no longer need to make decisions, solve problems, or engage in critical thinking. The act of thinking itself, the exercise of intellectual labor, has become outsourced to algorithms, to artificial intelligence, and to systems designed to anticipate our every need. This externalization of cognitive labor diminishes our capacity for independent thought, as we rely increasingly on pre-packaged solutions rather than engaging with the world directly.

Consider, for instance, the modern economy's reliance on platforms those invisible digital infrastructures that dictate the flow of information, commerce, and social interaction. Platforms, ostensibly designed to simplify our lives, have become pervasive gatekeepers, structuring not only our access to goods and services but our very interactions with the world. The choice of which product to purchase, which service to engage with, and even which viewpoint to consider is now mediated by platforms whose algorithms prioritize convenience and profitability over complexity and diversity. These platforms are not neutral facilitators; they are gatekeepers of our lives, shaping the way we think, interact, and behave.

The second cost is the decay of resilience. In a world where everything is engineered to be effortless, human beings lose the very capacities that once enabled them to navigate hardship and uncertainty. Resilience mental, emotional, and physical thrives in environments that challenge the individual, that force one to confront adversity, adapt, and persevere. Yet, in a society driven by the imperative of convenience, the very fabric of resilience is undermined. The more we simplify our world, the less we are forced to develop the fortitude required to endure discomfort or difficulty. In this context, individuals become increasingly fragile, unable to cope with even modest challenges that do not fit into the preordained structure of convenience. The reality is that ease breeds fragility an existence in which comfort is paramount, and the capacity for enduring adversity is atrophied.

This fragility is compounded by the attraction to instant gratification. The commodification of convenience has been intricately tied to the desire for immediate pleasure and the avoidance of delay or discomfort. From streaming services that provide instant access to entertainment, to food delivery apps that promise gourmet meals with little more than a few taps, the ability to have it all in an instant has led to an environment in which patience and deferred gratification have become alien concepts. The more immediate and easily obtainable pleasure becomes, the more incapable individuals become of enduring the long-term, often arduous, processes of delayed satisfaction and personal growth.

However, perhaps the most troubling cost of convenience is its subjugation of free will through the automation of choice. In the realm of consumerism, choice has long been heralded as a pillar of freedom the ability to select one's path, to determine one's desires, to assert one's independence through the act of consumption. Yet, with the advent of algorithms and predictive technologies, the illusion of free choice has become increasingly hollow. Platforms learn our preferences, anticipate our needs, and push us toward specific products, services, and ideologies. The notion that we are freely choosing our path becomes more illusory with each passing day, as we are herded along pre-determined channels, shaped by the invisible hand of data and algorithmic prediction. In this sense, the promise of convenience has become a form of manufactured freedom a freedom that exists only within the confines of what has been algorithmically determined to be acceptable or desirable.

This technological determinism the idea that technology, in its relentless advance, shapes and dictates human behavior has profound consequences for the way we understand individual agency. The more we rely on technology to make our decisions, the less we are able to trust ourselves to make those decisions independently. Our will is no longer free; it is shaped, subtly and invisibly, by the very tools that were designed to liberate us. The automation of choice, which began with simple conveniences such as recommending products or services, now extends to the way we think, vote, and even feel. In this world, the individual is reduced to a mere node in a network of consumption, driven not by their own will but by an intricate web of technological imperatives.

The pervasive spread of convenience also accelerates the commodification of time the reduction of every moment of existence into a unit of productivity or consumption. In an age where time is increasingly seen as a valuable resource to be optimized, every moment must be filled with some form of consumption, whether it be the consumption of information, entertainment, or products. The idea of simply being, of allowing oneself to exist without the pressure of constant productivity or consumption, is rendered foreign. Time itself is converted into a commodity, to be maximized, spent, and optimized. In doing so, the very essence of what it means to live fully, to experience life in its raw and unmediated form, is hollowed out, reduced to a series of consumable moments strung together by the relentless march of efficiency.

As the architecture of convenience continues to entrench itself in the daily lives of individuals, the broader implications for societal health are equally concerning. When ease and comfort become the sole organizing principles of life, a culture of disengagement arises. The complexity of human existence its struggles, its contradictions, its potential for growth is diminished. The desire for real connection, for meaningful interaction, for genuine human engagement, is replaced by a superficial semblance of connection, mediated by screens and platforms that promise convenience but deliver isolation. In this world, the rich tapestry of human experience is reduced to an endless loop of consumption, distraction, and fleeting satisfaction.

Yet, the most paradoxical element of this system is that while convenience promises to relieve us of burdens, it often creates new, more insidious burdens. In its quest to simplify life, convenience consolidates power in the hands of a few corporations and tech conglomerates, rendering individuals increasingly powerless. The convenience of having everything at one's fingertips is paired with the inconvenience of losing one's autonomy, agency, and, ultimately, one's sense of self. The very tools that are supposed to liberate us instead trap us in a cycle of passive consumption, where convenience is the gilded cage in which we willingly imprison ourselves.

To reclaim true agency, we must confront the tyranny of convenience. This is not a call to reject technology or progress, but rather to recognize that convenience, when wielded without mindfulness, undermines our very capacity for growth, resilience, and genuine freedom. The challenge, then, is not to seek a return to a more arduous, labor-intensive existence, but to seek a balance one in which the tools of convenience serve us, rather than reducing us to their servile subjects. Only by recognizing the cost of convenience can we begin to break free from its shackles and reclaim the autonomy and agency that have been quietly eroded in the name of ease.

take a break have a sip of moralty

The Spectacle of Existence: How Society's Obsession with Appearances Eclipses Substance

In the world that we inhabit, appearances have become the dominant form of reality, a reality increasingly manufactured, curated, and commodified by an all-pervasive spectacle. What we once understood as truth, authenticity, and integrity has been gradually replaced by a carefully constructed veneer of perfection, a veneer that serves the interests of power and wealth while obscuring the deeper, often uncomfortable, complexities of the human condition. The spectacle, in its many forms, has transcended its original role as mere entertainment or distraction; it is now the defining feature of modern existence, shaping the ways in which individuals perceive themselves and each other, and, more insidiously, shaping the very contours of social and political reality.

The spectacle, as it functions in the contemporary world, is not simply the realm of mass media, celebrity culture, or consumer advertising. It is, at its core, a manifestation of a deeper cultural transformation a transformation wherein image supersedes substance, and where the pursuit of visibility becomes synonymous with the pursuit of value. In a society where status is increasingly determined by one's ability to project an idealized self, authenticity becomes a casualty, replaced by an endless performance of carefully curated identities. The individual's worth is no longer measured by their deeds, thoughts, or virtues, but by the image they are able to project an image that conforms to the prevailing ideals of beauty, success, and aspiration.

This obsession with appearance has profound implications for both the individual and the collective. On the individual level, it breeds a form of existential dislocation, wherein the true self is subordinated to the demands of social validation. The individual, in this context, becomes not a subject with intrinsic worth, but a mere performer in an endless spectacle, constantly striving to meet the expectations of an audience that is simultaneously omnipresent and indifferent. Identity itself becomes a fluid, performative construct, shaped not by inner truth but by external pressures, by the need to conform to the ever-shifting ideals of what is considered desirable, acceptable, and valuable.

At the societal level, this obsession with appearances transforms the very nature of relationships, both personal and political. The rise of social media, in particular, has magnified this spectacle, providing a platform for the constant projection of curated identities and fabricated lives. What is presented online is not the reality of individuals' lives, but an idealized version a version that conforms to a set of aesthetic and social standards designed to attract attention, garner approval, and elicit admiration. In this digital age, being seen has become synonymous with being real, and the act of self-presentation has replaced genuine connection and self-expression.

The superficiality of this spectacle is exacerbated by the rise of consumerism, which offers the illusion of authenticity through the purchase of products and lifestyles. Brands, through targeted advertising and influencer marketing, have learned to sell not just goods, but identities. The acquisition of products becomes an act of self-definition, where the individual is invited to align themselves with a certain image, whether that be one of sophistication, rebellion, or affluence. The branding of identity, whether through fashion, technology, or experiences, has become the ultimate act of self-expression. Yet, in this commodified identity, there is no true self to be found only a set of externally imposed images that serve the interests of capital and consumption.

This commodification of identity has far-reaching consequences for the notion of authenticity. In a world dominated by appearances, the concept of authenticity has been hollowed out, reduced to a mere marketing tool. What was once understood as genuine rooted in personal experience, self-awareness, and moral integrity has been supplanted by the superficial notion of authenticity, which is defined by conformity to external expectations. Authenticity, in this sense, becomes just another commodity, marketed and sold to the highest bidder. The individual no longer seeks to cultivate an authentic self, but a self that is validated by the external gaze, by the consumption of brands and ideologies that grant the illusion of individuality without the substance of true independence.

Moreover, the spectacle of existence has profound political implications. As appearance supplants substance, the substance of political life itself becomes secondary to the image of political figures, parties, and movements. Politics is no longer about the substance of policy, ideology, or governance, but about the performance of leadership, the construction of an image that resonates with the electorate. The modern political sphere is less concerned with the intricacies of policy-making or the addressing of societal issues, and more preoccupied with the cultivation of an image that appears competent, charismatic, and aligned with popular sentiment. The result is a political system that is more akin to a media production than a space for rational deliberation and decision-making.

The obsession with appearance also permeates the world of business and economics. In the corporate world, the emphasis on image on brand, reputation, and market positioning often eclipses the underlying realities of the companies themselves. Financial statements, once the primary tool of evaluating a company's health, have been supplanted by the story that a company tells about itself, the image it projects to investors, consumers, and the public. In this world, the substance of a company's performance becomes less important than the image it cultivates in the marketplace. As a result, companies that are effectively hollow, that have little to offer beyond a polished image, can thrive, while those that focus on substance and innovation often struggle to gain traction in a world that values spectacle over reality.

The spectacle also plays a critical role in shaping social norms and cultural values. As societal ideals become increasingly rooted in appearance, there is less space for diversity of thought, identity, or expression. The pressure to conform to a certain image to meet the prescribed standards of beauty, success, and achievement creates a stifling uniformity that stifles creativity and intellectual engagement. In this world, what is celebrated is not the richness of human experience, with all its messiness, contradictions, and complexities, but a flattened, idealized version of life, one that can be packaged and consumed. The real becomes overshadowed by the ideal, and the human condition is reduced to a series of commodified images, each of which must conform to an external standard in order to be valued.

Yet, the spectacle of existence is not merely a passive force; it is actively created and perpetuated by the systems that benefit from it. Wealth, power, and media conglomerates all play a role in constructing and maintaining this spectacle. By perpetuating idealized images of success, beauty, and happiness, these forces create a world in which the pursuit of appearance becomes the primary mode of existence, eclipsing the pursuit of truth. The spectacle thus serves as both a tool of distraction and a mechanism of control, keeping individuals focused on external validation rather than on the deeper, more substantive questions of life, identity, and meaning.

The most pernicious aspect of the spectacle is that it fosters a culture of simulation, where the line between reality and illusion becomes increasingly blurred. The individual, no longer able to distinguish between the real and the fabricated, begins to live in a state of permanent performance, caught in a loop of self-presentation and self-reinvention, disconnected from the deeper, more authentic aspects of human existence. The quest for self-actualization becomes a quest for external validation, and the pursuit of happiness becomes a pursuit of image. In this world, being is no longer enough; one must constantly appear to be something more.

In order to break free from the tyranny of the spectacle, we must first reclaim the value of substance the internal, the genuine, the unvarnished. True existence lies not in how we are perceived, but in how we perceive ourselves, in our actions, thoughts, and interactions. The spectacle may dominate the surface of our lives, but it is the deeper currents of truth, integrity, and authenticity that must anchor us in reality. To resist the allure of the spectacle is to engage in a radical act of self-liberation one that demands not perfection, but honesty, not image, but substance. Only in this reclamation of the real can we begin to reclaim our humanity from the forces that seek to reduce it to a mere performance.

Seventeen

The Fragmentation of Reality: The Collapse of Consensus and the Death of Truth

In an age marked by unprecedented access to information, we are witnessing a profound crisis in the very fabric of shared reality. The ideological divisions that once seemed to mark the extremes of political discourse have now permeated every aspect of society, fracturing the collective consciousness into a myriad of competing narratives. This fragmentation of reality is not merely the result of diverse opinions or contrasting worldviews, but a deliberate strategy to undermine the very possibility of consensus. The destabilization of truth, once considered a cornerstone of social cohesion, has become the most potent tool in the hands of those who seek to maintain control through confusion and division.

The death of truth, in this context, is not a simple collapse of facts, but a multiplication of truths, each tailored to serve a specific agenda. In a society where information flows faster than ever, where each individual is bombarded with an infinite array of perspectives, the line between what is true and what is merely believable becomes increasingly difficult to discern. The complexity of the world is reduced to binary oppositions: good versus evil, left versus right, us versus them. This reductionism serves those in power, for it simplifies the world into digestible chunks that can be easily manipulated and controlled. Yet, in the process, the nuance, complexity, and richness of human experience are lost.

The proliferation of alternative facts, post-truth politics, and the relentless pursuit of ideological purity has created a fractured landscape in which the very concept of objective reality is under siege. On the one hand, the ascension of fake news, conspiracy theories, and deliberate disinformation campaigns has become a tool of mass manipulation. On the other hand, the explosion of niche media, tailored algorithms, and personalized digital feeds has resulted in a situation where every individual inhabits a reality that is at once hyperspecific and utterly isolated from others. The more we engage with the digital realm, the more our perceptions of the world are shaped by filters not just the filters of social media, but the filters of ideology, of confirmation bias, of cognitive dissonance. We are no longer citizens of a shared world, but inhabitants of fragmented echo chambers.

This process of fragmentation is not accidental. It is, in fact, the deliberate consequence of power structures that seek to control the narrative. By flooding the public sphere with a cacophony of voices some authentic, many distorted those in positions of power ensure that no single narrative prevails. This dispersion of truth creates a state of permanent confusion, wherein individuals are left to navigate a vast and often contradictory sea of information. In such an environment, the individual is left with few tools to discern fact from fiction, to navigate the deluge of perspectives that bombard them from every angle. Truth itself becomes a commodity, one that can be bought, sold, and manipulated for political or economic gain.

The fragmentation of reality is intricately tied to the erosion of social trust. Once the glue that held societies together, trust is now in short supply. Trust in institutions, trust in the media, trust in experts, and even trust in one another has been steadily corroded, replaced by cynicism, suspicion, and fear. This erosion of trust is not merely a symptom of a declining society, but a calculated outcome of a system that thrives on division and alienation. As people grow more distrustful, they become increasingly dependent on their own fragmented narratives, unable or unwilling to seek common ground with others. In a society where every individual is ensnared in their own bubble, the idea of a shared reality becomes anathema.

The implications of this disintegration of trust are far-reaching. At the level of governance, the collapse of trust in public institutions has created a vacuum in which populist demagogues, con artists, and authoritarian figures thrive. These figures prey on the fractured reality of society, exploiting divisions and amplifying fears to consolidate power. With trust in the media and traditional political structures at an all-time low, these figures craft narratives that bypass reasoned debate and appeal directly to the emotions and prejudices of the masses. In a fragmented world, they become the arbiters of truth, offering certainty in an uncertain age.

At the level of the individual, the collapse of trust leads to a crisis of identity. When shared social markers those collective symbols of truth, morality, and justice disintegrate, individuals are left to navigate the world alone, constructing their own truths out of fragments of information, experience, and emotion. The search for authenticity becomes an act of self-reinvention, where individuals are forced to continually reassemble their own identities from the scattered debris of competing narratives. In the absence of a coherent worldview, identity becomes a shifting, protean concept one that is subject to constant redefinition in response to the latest trend, the latest crisis, or the latest piece of sensational news.

This fragmented identity is exacerbated by the ubiquitous nature of the digital world. Social media, with its emphasis on instant gratification and performance, encourages individuals to present a carefully curated version of themselves to the world. The person who exists on Instagram or Twitter is often a far cry from the person who exists in real life a curated, idealized version that conforms to the expectations of others, to the demands of an audience, or to the pressures of an algorithm. As the digital realm becomes the primary space of social interaction, the self becomes increasingly fragmented, split between the real and the virtual, between the authentic and the constructed.

This fragmentation also permeates our understanding of community. The traditional sense of community, once built on shared values, common experiences, and mutual understanding, is gradually being replaced by a fragmented, atomized form of connection. Social media may provide the illusion of connection, but it often serves to isolate individuals even further, creating a world in which people interact with others not as individuals, but as avatars, as projections of their most polished selves. These avatars, though they may be linked by shared interests or ideologies, often fail to foster true human connection true solidarity. In a fragmented world, the bonds that once held people together have been replaced by tenuous, superficial connections, easily broken by ideological differences, political polarization, or the latest viral outrage.

As the fragmentation of reality deepens, the question arises: What can be done to restore a sense of shared truth and collective identity? The answer lies not in a return to the past or a nostalgia for a simpler time, but in the radical reconstruction of how we engage with information, how we build relationships, and how we conceive of truth itself. First and foremost, we must recognize that truth is not a monolithic, objective entity, but a dialogue a process of negotiation, of critical engagement, of shared inquiry. In a world where reality has been splintered into a thousand competing narratives, the key to rebuilding social trust and consensus lies in communication in the willingness to listen, to challenge, and to engage with the ideas and experiences of others.

The future of our collective reality, then, depends not on the restoration of an idealized past, but on the creation of a new form of shared truth one that is rooted in dialogue, diversity, and mutual respect. We must learn to accept that truth is not a static thing, but a living conversation, one that evolves as we confront the complexities of the world. In this conversation, every voice matters, but no one voice can dominate. It is only through the collective effort of many voices each with their own experiences, perspectives, and truths that we can hope to rebuild a shared reality capable of uniting us in our common humanity.

Eighteen

The Illusion of Progress: How Technological Utopianism Conceals the Dystopia Beneath

In the dizzying whirlwind of contemporary life, the relentless march of technology is often heralded as humanity's greatest triumph. The promise of a future shaped by artificial intelligence, automation, and biotech is invoked with a fervor akin to religious zeal. We are told that technology will free us from toil, eradicate disease, and usher in an age of unparalleled prosperity and enlightenment. And yet, beneath this glittering utopian vision lies a far more troubling reality a reality in which technology does not serve the human spirit, but seeks to reshape it in its own image.

The allure of technological utopianism is a potent force. It taps into the deepest desires of human beings: the desire for comfort, for immortality, for transcendence. The promises are seductive: a world in which poverty, hunger, and disease are relics of the past, a world in which artificial intelligence not only performs menial tasks but also understands and meets our deepest needs, a world in which we can augment our bodies, enhance our minds, and live indefinitely. In the face of these promises, the very notion of human limitation begins to feel like an outdated concept, a primitive relic of a bygone era.

Yet, this vision of progress rests on a series of dangerous assumptions assumptions that obfuscate the true nature of technological advancement and its consequences. The first of these assumptions is the idea that progress is inherently good, that the forward march of technology will always lead to a better world. This assumption, however, fails to account for the ways in which technology can be hijacked, repurposed, and manipulated to serve the interests of the few at the expense of the many. Technological development is not neutral; it is shaped by the values, ideologies, and power structures that drive it. While the vast majority of humanity may stand to benefit from certain innovations, these innovations are often co-opted by those with the power to shape their deployment, ensuring that the benefits accrue disproportionately to the wealthy and powerful.

Take, for example, the rise of automation. On the surface, automation promises to free individuals from the drudgery of labor, to allow people to pursue more creative, fulfilling lives. Yet, the reality is that automation is not equally distributed it is concentrated in industries where profit extraction is maximized. The workers who stand to lose the most from automation are often those at the bottom of the economic ladder: factory workers, service industry employees, and others whose livelihoods depend on jobs that are increasingly susceptible to being replaced by machines. Rather than liberating these individuals, automation exacerbates existing inequalities, as wealth and control over the means of production become concentrated in the hands of a small elite, while vast swaths of the population are left to languish in economic irrelevance.

This phenomenon is compounded by the rise of the gig economy, in which workers are increasingly treated as disposable assets, their labor fragmented into precarious, low-wage tasks mediated through digital platforms. Technology, once seen as a means of liberation, has instead become a tool of subjugation, creating a precarious class of workers who are constantly on the edge of financial ruin. The convenience and efficiency promised by the digital revolution have come at the cost of job security, worker rights, and social stability. The gig economy, far from offering freedom, shackles workers to a system that values their labor only insofar as it can be efficiently extracted, leaving them vulnerable to exploitation and economic instability.

Beyond the economic consequences, technological utopianism also obscures the ways in which surveillance and control are embedded within the very systems that are sold to us as solutions to society's ills. The rise of smart technologies from home assistants to biometric tracking devices—has been accompanied by a profound increase in state and corporate surveillance. These technologies, which are sold to consumers as tools for convenience and personalization, are in fact data-gathering mechanisms that track every aspect of our lives. What we eat, how we sleep, where we go, who we interact with all of this is collected, analyzed, and monetized by corporations with a vested interest in shaping our behavior.

This surveillance society is not just a product of consumer technologies, but of the broader political economy of data. The vast troves of personal data harvested by tech companies are used to create highly targeted algorithms that influence everything from our purchasing decisions to our political beliefs. In this context, the concept of privacy becomes a quaint anachronism, a relic of a pre-digital age. In its place, we have a world in which individuals are no longer seen as autonomous subjects, but as data points to be mined, analyzed, and manipulated.

In this environment, freedom itself begins to lose its meaning. The promise of technological liberation freedom from physical limitations, freedom from disease, freedom from work becomes increasingly hollow as the true cost of this freedom is revealed. For all the advances in technology, human agency is increasingly undermined. The more we depend on algorithms to make decisions for us, the less capacity we have to make those decisions ourselves. The more we turn over control of our lives to artificial intelligence, the more we lose the ability to shape our own destinies. Rather than liberating us, technology serves as a mechanism of control, steering us into predetermined patterns of consumption, behavior, and thought.

Perhaps the most dystopian element of this technological vision is the biotechnological revolution. The advent of genetic engineering, neural augmentation, and the possibility of life extension promises to erase the natural limits of human life. Yet, this vision raises profound ethical questions, questions that are often glossed over in the heady rush to embrace progress at any cost. If technology allows us to extend human life indefinitely, or even to reshape human nature itself, what becomes of our understanding of mortality, identity, and humanity? Who gets to decide what constitutes a "better" human being? Who controls the technology that can alter our very essence?

Moreover, the promise of biotechnological progress is once again marred by the realities of power and inequality. The ability to enhance human capacities, to live longer, healthier lives, or to genetically design offspring, will not be equally available to all. It is likely to be reserved for the elite, those with the wealth and resources to afford these life-altering interventions. As a result, a new form of genetic aristocracy could emerge, one in which access to the most advanced technologies becomes the defining marker of privilege and status. In this future, the gap between the haves and the have-nots is not merely economic, but biological a gulf between those who can afford to transcend the limitations of their human condition and those who are left behind.

In the face of these challenges, the notion of progress itself must be called into question. True progress cannot be measured solely by technological advancements or the accumulation of material wealth. Progress must be understood as a holistic concept, one that includes not only the development of new technologies but the cultivation of wisdom, empathy, and social responsibility. It must involve a rethinking of what it means to live a meaningful life, a life that is not defined by the constant pursuit of novelty and efficiency, but by the recognition of our shared humanity.

The illusion of progress, then, is not merely the product of technological advancements, but the result of a cultural shift a shift in which the value of human life is increasingly measured by its capacity for productivity, consumption, and adaptation to new technologies. In this world, the ideal of progress becomes a tool of subjugation rather than liberation, a mask that conceals the underlying realities of power, inequality, and exploitation. If we are to avoid the dystopia that looms on the horizon, we must redefine progress, not as the endless expansion of technological control, but as a return to human-centered values—values that prioritize autonomy, connection, and the well-being of all, not just the privileged few.

Nineteen

The Specter of Inequality: How the System Perpetuates Itself

Inequality whether in its economic, social, or political manifestations has long been an ever-present specter haunting the global landscape. In the contemporary era, however, inequality is no longer merely a background feature of societal structures; it has become a systemic condition, woven into the very fabric of our political and economic institutions. The gap between the affluent elite and the disenfranchised masses has reached unprecedented proportions, and yet, paradoxically, the systems that perpetuate this inequality are presented as the very engines of progress, freedom, and opportunity. Beneath the glossy narratives of meritocracy and upward mobility lies an intricate web of structures designed to preserve and entrench inequality, ensuring that the powerful remain entrenched in their dominion while the powerless are kept in a state of perpetual subjugation.

The most insidious aspect of inequality in modern society is its ability to disguise itself as fairness, to present itself as the natural consequence of individual effort, talent, and enterprise. The myth of the self-made individual the idea that anyone, regardless of background or circumstance, can rise through sheer willpower and merit pervades contemporary discourse. This myth serves a crucial function for the elites: it allows them to maintain their position of privilege while simultaneously obscuring the structural forces that have enabled their success. The affluent do not succeed because of their exceptional talents alone; they succeed because the system has been engineered to reward their success and to allocate resources in ways that perpetuate their dominance.

At the core of this system lies the concept of capital the accumulation of wealth, assets, and resources that provide access to opportunities and privileges unavailable to the majority. Capital, in this context, is not merely a function of hard work or entrepreneurial spirit, but the product of historical processes that have systematically concentrated wealth and power in the hands of a select few. From colonialism to corporate monopolies, from land ownership to inheritance, the systems that generate and maintain capital are inherently unequal. These systems are not neutral they are designed to ensure that the wealthy remain wealthy, that the powerful remain powerful, and that those at the bottom are locked into a cycle of poverty and disenfranchisement.

The notion that wealth is a direct result of individual effort is also central to the myth of meritocracy. In a society that prides itself on being a meritocratic system, the prevailing ideology suggests that anyone who works hard enough, studies diligently enough, or shows enough ambition will inevitably achieve success. This belief is intoxicating, for it promises the possibility of a fair and just society in which individuals are rewarded based on their abilities, not their birth or social position. Yet, beneath the surface, meritocracy is a myth a convenient fiction that obscures the ways in which social, racial, and economic privileges are passed down across generations.

The reality is that the playing field is far from level. The affluent have access to resources that the majority of people can only dream of: elite education, family connections, political influence, and financial capital. These advantages are often invisible to those who have not experienced them, creating a false sense of equality where none exists. The narrative of meritocracy suggests that those who do not succeed simply have not worked hard enough, or lack the necessary talent. This not only places the blame for failure on the individual, but it also masks the systemic inequities that shape one's opportunities in life. Those born into privilege are afforded opportunities and resources that those born into poverty could never access, regardless of their innate talents or work ethic. Thus, meritocracy functions as a powerful ideological tool that justifies and legitimizes inequality.

The myth of the self-made individual and the promise of meritocracy are further reinforced by the pervasive role of consumerism in modern society. Consumption, in the contemporary age, is not just an economic activity it is an expression of one's social worth, an outward symbol of personal success, and a means of achieving status. The affluent class, through their consumption patterns, further solidifies their social position, while the masses are encouraged to aspire to a lifestyle that is ultimately unattainable. Advertisements, social media influencers, and popular culture create an idealized image of success, one that is characterized not by personal fulfillment or community engagement, but by the accumulation of material goods and the projection of a certain image of wealth and power.

Yet, this consumerist ethos functions as a distraction, a diversionary tactic that keeps individuals focused on the superficial accumulation of goods rather than on addressing the deeper systemic issues of inequality. Consumption, in this sense, becomes a mechanism for control encouraging individuals to internalize their dissatisfaction, to compensate for their lack of power or agency by acquiring more goods or achieving a more polished image. This cycle of consumption not only fuels the economy but also perpetuates inequality by reinforcing the class structures that sustain it. Those who can afford to consume at the highest levels are able to further differentiate themselves from the lower classes, perpetuating a system of social stratification that discourages the possibility of upward mobility.

Another critical dimension of inequality is the role of political power in maintaining the status quo. The wealthy elite have not only accumulated economic capital, but they have also amassed significant political power, which they wield to protect their interests and ensure the continuation of a system that benefits them. Through lobbying, campaign donations, and the revolving door between politics and business, the affluent exert disproportionate influence over government policy. Laws and regulations that are designed to protect workers, the environment, or the public good are often shaped by corporate interests that seek to maximize profits and minimize costs, often at the expense of the public. This unequal access to political power ensures that the policies that shape society tax laws, labor regulations, environmental protections are crafted to perpetuate the dominance of the wealthy.

Moreover, the political system itself has become increasingly corporatized, with politicians and public officials often having more in common with the business elites they purport to regulate than with the people they represent. In such a system, political power becomes a tool of the elite, used to safeguard their wealth and power while maintaining the illusion of democratic representation. Elections become a spectacle a performance in which the public is invited to choose between candidates who are, in essence, the same—who share the same interests and who are financed by the same wealthy donors. In this context, political change becomes little more than a pantomime, a superficial exercise that masks the deeper forces of inequality that continue to shape society.

Furthermore, inequality is perpetuated through the insidious forces of intergenerational transmission. Wealth and privilege are passed down from one generation to the next, often in ways that are invisible to the public eye. Inheritance, for instance, allows the affluent to retain and grow their wealth across generations, while the poor are left with little more than the opportunity to work themselves into the ground for a lifetime. The fact that inheritance plays such a critical role in maintaining social stratification demonstrates that the system is rigged, that the deck is stacked in favor of those who are born into privilege. In this way, inequality is not merely a result of individual failings or lack of effort, but a structural condition that is perpetuated through the very mechanisms of society.

Inequality, then, is not a natural or inevitable condition, but a manufactured one a system that is deliberately constructed and perpetuated by those with the power to shape it. It is sustained by myths that obscure the true nature of wealth and success, by political structures that serve the interests of the elite, and by economic systems that reward the accumulation of capital while penalizing those who lack it. To address inequality, it is not enough to simply redistribute wealth or raise wages; we must fundamentally rethink the systems that underpin it. We must dismantle the ideologies of meritocracy and the myths of self-made success, and confront the deeply entrenched power structures that preserve inequality. Only then can we begin to build a more just and equitable society one that recognizes the inherent worth of every individual, regardless of their social standing or economic position.

Twenty

The Anatomy of Control: How Power Manipulates the Masses

In the labyrinth of modern governance, where the mechanics of influence are finely tuned and expertly hidden, the masses are increasingly entangled in webs of manipulation so intricate that they scarcely recognize their own subjugation. Power whether vested in institutions, corporations, or clandestine networks no longer operates in overt displays of force, but in the subtle art of indirect control. The tools of coercion are no longer chains and locks, but the seemingly benign forces of consumerism, distraction, ideation, and emotion. The architecture of modern control is built not on brute force but on the more insidious mechanisms of persuasion, normalization, and invisibility, leaving the average individual unknowingly complicit in their own subjugation.

The first principle of control lies in the creation of perceived scarcity. A system designed to keep people perpetually wanting, always striving for more, is one in which the illusion of scarcity becomes a powerful lever of manipulation. In a world of technological abundance and global connectivity, the vast majority of human needs could theoretically be met without the overwhelming inequalities we observe. Yet, the manufacture of scarcity serves to perpetuate an economic system that benefits the few at the expense of the many. Through a careful orchestration of supply chains, market monopolies, and deliberate restrictions on access, those in control ensure that what could be universally available remains tantalizingly out of reach for most. This manufactured scarcity extends beyond the material and into the psychological. By stoking an insatiable desire for more .More wealth, more status, more possessions the system keeps individuals locked in a constant state of dissatisfaction, driving them to expend ever greater energy and resources in the pursuit of what is always just beyond their grasp.

This illusion of scarcity is carefully maintained by the second mechanism of control: pervasive distraction. The modern individual is bombarded from every direction with stimuli designed to deflect attention away from the core realities of their existence. From the ceaseless churn of news cycles to the addictive pull of social media, from the siren song of celebrity culture to the all-consuming allure of consumer goods, the individual is kept in a state of perpetual distraction. The aim is simple: to ensure that people remain focused on the trivial and the superficial, so that they are unable to reflect critically on their own circumstances, on the systems that perpetuate their discontent, or on the profound inequalities that govern their lives. The more attention is directed outward, the less energy is available for the inward reflection necessary to challenge the status quo.

This distraction is also tied to the cultivation of passivity in the population. It is no accident that the most opulent and powerful sectors of society often promote ideologies of individualism, personal responsibility, and self-reliance. While these ideals are presented as pathways to personal fulfillment and success, they simultaneously absolve the system itself of responsibility. The individual is told that their success or failure is a result of their own efforts, and that any failure to achieve is the consequence of their own inadequacy. This ideological framework serves to depoliticize the population, convincing individuals that their lot in life is entirely the product of personal choice, and that collective action or systemic change is unnecessary or even counterproductive. By internalizing this narrative, the masses are diverted from the structural forces of oppression that dictate the terms of their existence.

In this climate of distraction and internalized blame, the system employs yet another tool of control: the manipulation of fear. Fear, whether of economic collapse, social unrest, or the loss of personal status, is one of the most effective means of securing compliance. Those in power understand that fear not only immobilizes individuals but also directs them towards scapegoats, creating divisions among the populace that prevent collective resistance. The media, political rhetoric, and corporate interests all capitalize on the human proclivity for fear, amplifying perceived threats whether through sensationalized news stories or the strategic cultivation of ideological enemies—in order to divert attention from the true sources of insecurity. In this way, fear becomes a weapon of distraction, a tool to fragment solidarity and keep the public at odds with one another rather than with the systems of power that sustain their oppression.

The next stage in the anatomy of control is the use of ideology a system of ideas that shapes perception, constructs meaning, and justifies the existing order. Ideology is not simply a matter of political theory; it is the air we breathe, the lens through which we interpret our world, and the framework within which our actions make sense. Through the power of ideology, the status quo is presented as natural, inevitable, and even desirable. The pervasive mantra of "economic growth" is one such example growth for its own sake, regardless of the social, environmental, or ethical costs. Growth, under this paradigm, is not just an economic imperative but a moral one. The ideology of growth masks the fact that it is a deeply flawed system, one that relentlessly extracts from the earth and from human labor, pushing both to their breaking points.

Ideology works in tandem with the creation of false consciousness. By perpetuating narratives that justify existing inequalities, the dominant power structures ensure that those who are oppressed come to believe in their own powerlessness. This false consciousness is reinforced through media, education, and cultural institutions, which offer a version of reality that prioritizes individual achievement over collective well-being, wealth accumulation over social justice, and consumer satisfaction over environmental sustainability. The masses are encouraged to internalize these beliefs, to see themselves as failures if they do not succeed within this system, and to regard the system itself as beyond critique.

Another critical mechanism of control is the normalization of inequality. Over time, social and economic disparities are naturalized and rendered invisible, no longer seen as the result of specific political or economic decisions but as inherent features of the human condition. This normalization occurs through the systematic erasure of history, the marginalization of dissenting voices, and the dehumanization of those who suffer most from inequality. When inequality becomes "normal," it is no longer questioned, and those who suffer from it are stigmatized as responsible for their own plight. This normalization occurs on both a micro and macro level at the level of individual relationships, where the affluent are normalized as "better" or more deserving, and at the societal level, where structural oppression is erased from the public discourse.

The final mechanism of control is the cultivation of complacency. Over time, the system is designed to encourage individuals to accept their station, to "know their place" and cease striving for more. The system of inequality, in its most sophisticated form, generates a pervasive apathy in the population an apathy that is fueled by the overwhelming complexity and intractability of the systems that govern their lives. When the individual becomes convinced that they are powerless to effect change, they resign themselves to their fate. This resignation, often seen in the apathy towards politics, social movements, or collective action, serves as the final safeguard against resistance. In this way, the system perpetuates itself, as individuals, exhausted by their struggles and overwhelmed by the seeming futility of action, acquiesce to their subjugation.

Yet, while these mechanisms of control are powerful, they are not invincible. Every system of control depends on a delicate balance between the rulers and the ruled, and this balance can be disrupted. The moment of rupture occurs when the controlled begin to question the very systems that have shaped their existence. When the illusion of scarcity breaks, when the distraction no longer holds, when the fear no longer manipulates, when the ideology becomes transparent, and when the complacency of the masses shatters, the system of control is in jeopardy. The question, then, is not whether this rupture will occur, but when and what forms of resistance will emerge in its wake.

Twenty one

The Spectacle of Consent: How Power Manufactures Compliance

In the heart of modern society, where the narratives of freedom, democracy, and individual autonomy are enshrined as sacred truths, there lies a paradox as insidious as it is invisible. For all the rhetoric of personal liberty and collective governance, the majority of individuals live in a system of manufactured consent a system where compliance is not only achieved through force or coercion, but through the more subtle, yet equally powerful, mechanisms of consensus-building, legitimization, and psychological manipulation. In this labyrinth of influence, those at the top do not merely dictate from above; they craft the conditions under which the masses come to believe that their subjugation is not only inevitable but desirable.

At the core of this manufactured consent is the deliberate construction of a narrative a story about the world, about society, about power that is designed to make the existing order appear natural, legitimate, and even just. This narrative is not merely a matter of political propaganda or media spin; it is embedded in every aspect of social life, from the educational systems that shape young minds, to the cultural norms that dictate behavior, to the economic systems that structure one's opportunities and desires. It is a narrative that permeates the very air we breathe, a quiet hum of unquestioned truths that dictate how we perceive ourselves, our place in the world, and the systems that govern our lives.

The art of manufacturing consent is an intricate one, and it hinges on the creation of a false consensus the idea that the majority of people share the same values, desires, and goals as those who hold power. In truth, of course, this consensus is not organic; it is carefully cultivated through a variety of mechanisms, all of which serve to shape public opinion and steer it in directions that benefit the elites. The key to this manufactured consensus is the idea of social conformity, the subtle pressure to align one's thoughts, beliefs, and actions with the prevailing norms, even when these norms work against one's own interests.

One of the most effective tools in this process is the media, which serves as the gatekeeper of information, filtering and shaping the narratives that reach the public. The media, far from being an impartial observer, acts as an active participant in the construction of consent. By framing issues in certain ways, by highlighting specific events while ignoring others, by presenting a narrow range of perspectives as though they represent the full spectrum of thought, the media creates a reality that appears to be objective and consensual, when in fact it is shaped and distorted by powerful interests. The mass media television, newspapers, social media platforms, and digital outlets serve not only as purveyors of information but as architects of public perception.

Consider, for example, the ways in which economic crises are framed. In times of economic downturn, it is not unusual for the media to focus on the behaviors of individuals, attributing the crisis to personal irresponsibility, lack of foresight, or poor decision-making. Rarely do we hear about the structural causes of these crises the manipulation of markets, the collusion of financial institutions, the deregulation of industries, or the predatory behavior of global corporations. By placing the blame on individuals, the media serves to deflect attention from the real perpetrators of economic harm and, in doing so, reinforces the narrative of individual responsibility, while absolving the system itself from culpability.

Moreover, the media does not merely present a biased version of reality; it also manufactures desires. Through advertising, entertainment, and the cultivation of celebrity culture, the media teaches us what to want, what to aspire to, and what constitutes a successful or meaningful life. The mass media's role in shaping our desires is not incidental; it is an essential part of the system of control. The constant bombardment of images, symbols, and messages creates a consumer culture in which satisfaction is always just out of reach. We are encouraged to strive for more possessions, more status, more validation while the deeper, more existential questions of meaning, purpose, and community are ignored or trivialized.

The media is not alone in this endeavor. The education system, which purports to be the great equalizer and the vehicle of social mobility, is itself a tool of manufactured consent. From an early age, individuals are taught to accept the rules of the game, to internalize the values of the dominant class, and to see their own success or failure as the result of individual effort, rather than systemic forces. Education, in this sense, functions not to liberate the mind but to discipline it, to teach young people how to fit into the existing social order. The curriculum, textbooks, and standardized testing all reinforce a narrow conception of knowledge, one that prioritizes conformity over critical thinking, obedience over autonomy, and competition over collaboration.

This is not to say that education cannot be a force for empowerment; indeed, it is through education that individuals have the potential to break free from the chains of manufactured consent. But in its current form, the education system often works in tandem with other institutions to perpetuate a certain worldview one that justifies inequality, reinforces hierarchy, and normalizes the status quo. By teaching students to accept the existing social order as natural and inevitable, education helps to ensure that the next generation will be just as complicit in the maintenance of power as the one before it.

A third crucial mechanism in the creation of consent is the political system itself. In democratic societies, elections are heralded as the highest expression of popular sovereignty, a chance for the people to choose their leaders and shape the direction of their nation. However, the illusion of democracy is only possible if the system remains closed if the choices presented to voters are within a narrowly defined range of acceptable options. In this sense, the political system does not offer true choice but rather a selection of options that all serve the same basic interests. The candidates, though they may represent different parties, are often backed by the same corporate sponsors, share the same broad ideological framework, and work within the same economic system. In this way, elections become less about real power and more about maintaining the appearance of democracy.

Moreover, the political process itself is dominated by elite interests, whose access to wealth, media, and lobbying power ensures that their voices are heard above all others. The vast majority of the population, despite their right to vote, remains largely excluded from the political decision-making process, as their concerns are sidelined in favor of those with the resources to shape policy. This electoral capture ensures that, while the people may have the form of democratic participation, they do not have its substance. Elections become rituals of consent, where the illusion of choice allows the powerful to claim legitimacy while perpetuating a system that serves only their interests.

As the processes of consent manufacture become more sophisticated, so too does the psychological manipulation of the individual. In a society where information is omnipresent and attention is fragmented, individuals often experience a profound sense of powerlessness. The complexity of global systems, the overwhelming barrage of information, and the rapid pace of change create an environment in which people feel as though their voices are drowned out, their actions insignificant, and their futures uncertain. In response, the individual is not encouraged to resist or challenge the system, but to retreat into personal consumption, entertainment, and identity politics all of which serve to distract, pacify, and isolate.

The system's success lies not in the direct exercise of force, but in its ability to make individuals believe they are free, even as they are controlled. The spectacle of consent is a performance a carefully orchestrated production that makes the masses complicit in their own subjugation. By shaping desires, influencing beliefs, and providing a false sense of agency, power has created a society in which the very act of resisting seems not only futile but unnatural. In this way, those who would seek to disrupt the system find themselves not only opposed by the powerful but alienated from their peers, who have internalized the system's values and beliefs.

Thus, the true nature of control in the modern world is not to impose obedience through overt force, but to manufacture consent, to shape reality in such a way that the individual willingly submits to the system, even as they believe they are choosing to do so. It is this subtle, pervasive form of control where power and compliance are indistinguishable that is the most dangerous, for it leaves no room for rebellion, no space for dissent, and no possibility for true liberation.

Twenty two

The Alchemy of Obscurity: How Information is Weaponized

In the digital age, where knowledge is ostensibly more accessible than ever before, the paradox of information overload and knowledge scarcity persists as one of the most potent tools in the arsenal of the powerful. Information, once considered the currency of democracy and the bedrock of enlightenment, has become an instrument of obfuscation a weapon wielded not to empower, but to confuse, control, and manipulate. In this alchemical process, information is no longer the transparent conduit to truth, but rather a murky, distorted medium that serves the interests of those who control its flow. The result is a world where clarity has become a rare commodity, and the public, rather than being liberated by knowledge, is mired in the fog of competing narratives, sensationalism, and manufactured crises.

The first tenet of this alchemical transformation of information is the deliberate creation of ambiguity. In an era where access to data is ubiquitous, the sheer volume of information available to the public should, in theory, foster a more informed and engaged populace. Yet, as the floodgates of information have opened, they have also drowned individuals in a cacophony of contradictory sources, each vying for attention and validation. In this environment, the ability to discern fact from fiction, truth from distortion, becomes increasingly elusive. The vast expanse of information is carefully curated by those in power to ensure that ambiguity prevails, so that no single narrative dominates and no clarity emerges. This manipulation of information ensures that individuals remain in a perpetual state of confusion, unable to challenge the status quo because they are unsure of the very facts upon which they might base their resistance.

Consider the modern media landscape, where an infinite number of news outlets, blogs, and social media platforms provide contradictory accounts of the same event. One report claims that economic austerity measures are necessary to restore financial stability, while another argues that they are a thinly veiled strategy to shift wealth to the rich. One headline decries the growing inequality in society, while another celebrates the burgeoning prosperity of a select few. The result is a media environment in which the line between fact and opinion becomes increasingly blurred. The power of the media elite lies not in the truth they disseminate, but in the uncertainty they cultivate. By controlling the narrative, the media can dictate the terms of debate, forcing the public to grapple with the illusion of equal, yet contradictory, truths. The citizen is no longer presented with clear, discernible facts upon which they can base informed decisions but is instead left to navigate an ocean of noise, where every wave of information seems equally valid, yet equally shallow.

The second aspect of this information warfare is the strategic use of distraction. In an age of constant connectivity, individuals are inundated with a relentless stream of information news, social media updates, advertising, entertainment each vying for their attention. This saturation of stimuli ensures that critical issues, those that might challenge the entrenched power structures, are relegated to the background, overshadowed by the latest viral trend, celebrity scandal, or political drama. In this environment, the powerbrokers do not need to overtly suppress information they need only to divert attention. By focusing the public's gaze on trivial matters, they ensure that the more pressing issues the ones that might lead to systemic change are ignored, forgotten, or dismissed as too complex or distant.

The phenomenon of clickbait is a perfect example of this distractionary tactic. Headlines designed to provoke curiosity, outrage, or amusement generate millions of clicks, but the content often bears little substantive relation to the promise made by the headline. In this way, the public's attention is directed toward superficial, easily digestible content that satisfies fleeting emotional needs, but which leaves little room for reflection, analysis, or action. This process reduces the citizenry to passive consumers, devouring content in the same way they consume products, rather than active participants in the formation of their social and political reality.

In a similar vein, the strategic use of misinformation serves as another weapon in the manipulation of public consciousness. The deliberate spread of false or misleading information whether through fabricated stories, doctored images, or misleading statistics has become an increasingly effective tool of control. By muddying the waters of public discourse, those in power can distort the facts and obscure the truth, ensuring that the populace is left with a fragmented and confused understanding of reality. The rise of deepfakes highly convincing falsifications of videos and audio recordings has only exacerbated this problem, blurring the lines between reality and fabrication to a degree that makes it increasingly difficult for the average citizen to trust their own senses.

However, the manipulation of information is not restricted to the realm of media or digital spaces; it extends into the very architecture of knowledge production itself. The academy, long seen as a bastion of intellectual inquiry and objective analysis, has itself become enmeshed in the mechanisms of power. The proliferation of corporate sponsorships, research grants, and political lobbying within universities has created an environment in which academic institutions, rather than acting as neutral forums for the free exchange of ideas, have become co-opted by corporate and governmental interests. This phenomenon, known as academic capture, ensures that the research agendas of universities align with the priorities of their financiers, distorting the very nature of knowledge production. Research that challenges the status quo, whether in the fields of climate science, economics, or social justice, is marginalized, while studies that support the prevailing orthodoxy are elevated and disseminated.

This distortion of knowledge is also evident in the way in which certain voices are systematically excluded from public discourse. Dissent whether in the form of critical journalism, activist movements, or alternative academic perspectives is often relegated to the margins, framed as radical, unrealistic, or dangerous. This ideological exclusion is not always a matter of overt censorship but often takes the form of subtle suppression. Dissenting voices are ignored, misrepresented, or vilified, creating the illusion of unanimity around the dominant worldview. In this context, the so-called "free market of ideas" is not an open arena of contestation, but a highly regulated space in which only certain ideas are allowed to circulate freely, while others are confined to the shadows.

Moreover, the systematic discrediting of alternative narratives ensures that those who challenge the prevailing order are not only ignored but actively undermined. Activists, independent journalists, and intellectuals who dare to question the power structures that dominate society are branded as conspiracy theorists, ideologues, or extremists. This smear campaign serves to delegitimize dissent, casting those who question the system as irrational or dangerous, while reinforcing the legitimacy of the powers that be. In this way, the entire landscape of information is shaped to ensure that the status quo remains unchallenged.

One of the most insidious aspects of this information war is its ability to foster a sense of learned helplessness. By continually presenting contradictory narratives, distracting the public with trivialities, and undermining alternative viewpoints, the system creates a climate in which individuals feel powerless to effect change. The sheer complexity of the world, coupled with the overwhelming flood of information, leads many to retreat into a state of apathy or resignation. If everything is a matter of interpretation, if all truths are equally contested, then why bother seeking out the truth at all? In this way, the bombardment of information itself becomes a mechanism of control, fostering a sense of inertia and passivity that makes resistance seem not only futile but irrational.

the alchemy of obscurity the process by which information is distorted, diluted, and disempowered serves as a critical tool in maintaining control. By creating ambiguity, distracting the public, spreading misinformation, co-opting knowledge production, and discrediting dissent, those in power ensure that the masses remain uninformed, disoriented, and ultimately complicit in their own subjugation. The question remains: how can we reclaim the power of information and transform it from a tool of control into a means of liberation? The answer lies not in simply amassing more data, but in developing the critical faculties necessary to navigate this labyrinth of deception and uncover the truths that lie hidden beneath the surface.

Twenty three

The Mirage of Sovereignty: How Power Alters Perception of Freedom

One of the most insidious illusions of the modern world is the notion of sovereignty the idea that individuals, communities, or even entire nations are free to shape their own destinies, to make decisions independent of external influence. In theory, sovereignty embodies the very essence of liberty. It suggests a realm of self-determination, where the will of the people, the desires of the individual, and the autonomy of the collective are supreme. Yet, beneath this lofty ideal lies a complex and often unseen machinery, quietly reconfiguring the very contours of freedom and governance. The modern state, no matter how democratic it may appear on the surface, is often little more than a theater a carefully constructed performance designed to convince the public of their agency while subtly ensuring that real power lies elsewhere.

At the heart of this illusion of sovereignty is the role of centralized authority, which, through various forms of regulation, bureaucracy, and legislation, claims the mantle of protector and arbiter of individual rights. On paper, the state exists to safeguard the freedom of its citizens to provide security, to maintain order, and to mediate between competing interests. Yet, as with any illusion, the deeper one looks into the workings of the state, the more apparent it becomes that its true role is often not to empower the people, but to manage and regulate their freedom in ways that benefit those who hold the reins of power. Through subtle mechanisms of control be it economic policy, legal frameworks, or military interventions the state orchestrates the appearance of freedom, while simultaneously curbing its true potential.

The central myth perpetuated by modern governance is that political participation whether through voting, protesting, or engaging in public discourse is the primary means through which sovereignty is expressed. In democratic societies, elections are heralded as the highest expression of popular will. Citizens are encouraged to believe that their participation in the electoral process is the defining act of their sovereignty, that by casting a ballot, they are directly shaping the future of their nation. But in reality, the act of voting, though it appears as an exercise in freedom, is often little more than an illusion of choice. The candidates and parties presented to the electorate are, for the most part, locked in a narrow ideological spectrum, all of which operate within the confines of an economic and political system that serves the interests of the wealthy and powerful. The political system itself is a closed loop, designed to maintain the status quo rather than challenge it.

This narrowing of choice is not accidental; it is by design. The true architects of power are not the candidates or politicians whom the people vote for, but the unseen forces corporate elites, financial institutions, and shadowy conglomerates who shape the platforms, policies, and discourse of the political establishment. The superficial choice between different political parties obscures the fact that all these options are ultimately bound by the same economic constraints and ideological assumptions. This engineered convergence of political options ensures that, regardless of who occupies the seats of power, the underlying structures of inequality, injustice, and exploitation remain intact.

Furthermore, economic sovereignty, or the ability to control one's own financial destiny, has been systematically undermined by the very forces that claim to protect freedom. The global economy, governed by multinational corporations, trade agreements, and financial institutions, is structured in such a way that true economic autonomy is rendered nearly impossible. Workers are trapped in a cycle of wage labor, indebtedness, and dependency, while corporations often global in scale and influence manipulate markets, extract resources, and evade taxation through sophisticated networks of legal loopholes and offshore havens. The apparent freedom of the marketplace is nothing more than a carefully orchestrated simulation, designed to give the illusion of open competition, while in reality, it consolidates wealth and power in the hands of a few.

Even the language of freedom itself is weaponized. Liberalism, which once championed the rights of individuals to be free from state coercion, has been co-opted into a hollow mantra, used to justify policies that perpetuate inequality and the concentration of power. In this warped version of liberalism, freedom is defined not by the liberation of the oppressed or the dismantling of entrenched systems of power, but by the ability of individuals to compete in the marketplace regardless of the social, economic, or environmental consequences of that competition. The so-called "freedom" of the individual in this context is reduced to a transactional relationship in which one's worth is measured solely by their capacity to accumulate wealth, influence, and status.

In the realm of global politics, this illusion of sovereignty is even more pronounced. The myth of national self-determination has been systematically eroded by the rise of transnational corporations, international financial institutions, and global trade agreements. Sovereign nations, once seen as autonomous entities with the ability to chart their own course, are increasingly subjugated to the dictates of global capital. Through mechanisms such as austerity measures, trade wars, and the manipulation of currency, global financial institutions exert control over the policies and economies of sovereign states. The political autonomy of nations is thus compromised, as they find themselves bound by the imperatives of international finance, often to the detriment of their own citizens.

This international corporatocracy an unholy alliance of multinational corporations, financial institutions, and international organizations has supplanted the idea of sovereign states with the concept of economic empires. These empires are not defined by borders or national identities, but by the vast networks of capital that flow across them. In these new economic empires, the sovereignty of individual nations is subordinated to the interests of global capital. Nations are left with little room for independent action, as they are coerced into adopting policies that align with the priorities of multinational corporations and international financial institutions.

Even within this globalized framework, social
sovereignty the ability of communities to govern
their own lives and protect their own interests is
systematically undermined. The corporate capture
of public services, such as healthcare, education,
and infrastructure, has shifted the balance of
power away from the people and into the hands of
profit-driven entities. In this new paradigm, the
health and well-being of individuals are treated as
commodities to be bought and sold, rather than as
fundamental human rights. Communities that once
had control over their own local economies,
resources, and services now find themselves
beholden to corporate interests that dictate the
terms of their existence.

Yet, despite these overwhelming forces, the illusion
of sovereignty persists, and with it, the illusion of
freedom. In a world where choice, independence,
and liberty are increasingly circumscribed, people
continue to believe that they are free because they
can vote, because they can consume, because they
can participate in the marketplace of ideas. The
true freedom the freedom to govern one's own
life, to determine one's own future, to live without
the looming shadow of corporate and state control

remains a distant dream, obscured by the shimmering veil of false sovereignty.

The question, then, is how we might break free from this mirage. How can we dismantle the structures of power that perpetuate the illusion of freedom while ensuring that true sovereignty political, economic, and social can once again become a tangible and lived reality? The path toward liberation lies in recognizing sovereignty for what it truly is: not an abstract concept, but a lived experience, rooted in the collective will of individuals who reclaim their agency, reject the falsehoods of the marketplace, and demand a world in which true freedom can flourish. Until we challenge the very definition of sovereignty itself until we question the assumptions that underpin our concept of freedom we will remain ensnared by the mirage that has been carefully constructed for us, and we will never taste the full potential of human liberty.

Twenty four

The Surrender of Autonomy: How The Mind Becomes The Final Battleground

In the age of unprecedented technological advancement and ubiquitous surveillance, the battlefield of power has shifted. No longer confined to physical borders or economic institutions, the war for control has now permeated the most intimate realm of human existence: the mind. The concept of autonomy, once heralded as the cornerstone of individual liberty, has been systematically eroded, not through overt force, but through the subtler, more insidious mechanisms of psychological manipulation, media saturation, and the commodification of identity. The battle is not merely one of wealth or governance it is a struggle for the very agency of the human psyche.

At its core, the surrender of autonomy begins with the subtle reshaping of perception. The human mind is not merely a passive receiver of information, but a complex processing center capable of critical thinking, analysis, and self-determination. However, this cognitive capacity, which has historically been viewed as the bedrock of human freedom, is increasingly being hijacked by external forces that seek to mold, manipulate, and engineer desire. Advertising, social media algorithms, political propaganda, and consumer culture each of these mechanisms has evolved to exploit the psychological vulnerabilities of the individual, shaping not just actions, but thoughts, desires, and ultimately, identity itself.

The modern advertising industry, with its multi-billion-dollar budget, has perfected the art of manipulation, employing sophisticated psychological tactics designed to bypass the rational mind and target the subconscious. Advertising does not simply sell products; it sells identities, aspirations, and ideologies. It creates a world in which consumption becomes a means of self-expression, a vehicle for constructing an idealized version of the self. Through relentless repetition and emotional appeal, advertisements transform consumer choices into markers of personal worth. In this way, individuals are no longer motivated by need or rational choice, but by a manufactured desire to attain the lifestyle, the status, or the happiness that the ad promises. The mind becomes the target, and the individual, instead of exercising free will, becomes a conduit for the desires implanted by unseen forces.

Yet, this is not a simple act of manipulation. The modern psyche is deeply interconnected with the vast digital infrastructure that surrounds it. Social media platforms, which have come to dominate the landscape of human interaction, serve as prime arenas for the commodification of personal identity. These platforms, ostensibly designed to connect people, have become powerful tools for the amplification of specific narratives, the distortion of reality, and the reinforcement of social norms. Algorithms, programmed to maximize engagement, create an environment in which the individual is bombarded with an unrelenting stream of content designed to trigger emotional responses, reinforce pre-existing beliefs, and shape behavior. The posts, images, and videos that one encounters are not random; they are carefully curated based on a vast network of data about one's preferences, habits, and psychological profile.

This process of digital curation has significant consequences for the autonomy of the individual. The more an individual interacts with these platforms, the more their preferences are fed back to them in a self-reinforcing loop. The result is an experience of confirmation bias, in which the mind becomes trapped within a narrow frame of reference, exposed only to ideas and opinions that align with its existing beliefs. This creates not only an ideological echo chamber but a psychological prison, where the individual is prevented from encountering new ideas or perspectives that might challenge their worldview. In this sense, the mind, once the seat of independent thought, becomes a passive receiver of pre-packaged beliefs and narratives that conform to the desires of those who control the digital ecosystem.

The consequence of this manipulation extends beyond the political or ideological realm it reaches deep into the fabric of personal identity. The individual, increasingly submerged in the curated reality of social media, becomes preoccupied with the need for external validation. The pursuit of "likes," "followers," and "shares" becomes not just a superficial form of social interaction, but the currency through which self-worth is measured. The need for constant affirmation transforms the individual from a sovereign agent into a subject of external influence, driven not by intrinsic values or personal goals, but by the desire to conform to the ever-shifting standards of online approval. This surrender of autonomy, in its most insidious form, occurs when the individual becomes trapped in a cycle of self-representation that is dictated not by their own values, but by the metrics and algorithms that drive the digital world.

However, this psychological conquest is not limited to the individual. The manipulation of collective thought, the shaping of social narratives, and the molding of public opinion have become central strategies for consolidating power in the modern world. The political landscape, increasingly dominated by media-savvy elites and powerful interest groups, exploits the psychological vulnerabilities of the public. Through targeted campaigns, fear-mongering, and emotional appeals, political entities manufacture consent and manipulate the collective will, guiding the masses toward decisions that serve the interests of the few.

One of the most striking examples of this manipulation is the rise of populism, which often capitalizes on the emotional and irrational aspects of the human psyche. Rather than engaging with complex issues through rational debate, populist leaders frequently resort to simple, emotive language that taps into deep-seated fears, anxieties, and prejudices. These leaders promise easy solutions to complex problems, exploiting the desires of their followers to feel empowered, validated, and in control. In this way, the public is not encouraged to engage in thoughtful deliberation, but rather to follow the lead of charismatic figures who promise them a return to an imagined golden age of sovereignty and control.

This psychological manipulation is facilitated by the tools of modern media, which have become increasingly sophisticated in their ability to shape the public's emotional responses. The 24-hour news cycle, with its constant barrage of sensationalist headlines, exaggerated narratives, and moral panics, ensures that the public's attention is constantly diverted toward crises and emergencies, real or imagined. In this environment, rational discourse is drowned out by the noise of fear and outrage. The result is a collective psyche that is perpetually on edge, constantly reacting to stimuli rather than engaging in proactive, critical thought. The surrender of autonomy, in this case, occurs not through overt coercion, but through the manipulation of emotions and the creation of a pervasive sense of urgency that stifles reasoned reflection.

It is in this climate of psychological warfare that the final battleground for true autonomy is fought. The mind, once considered the sanctuary of personal freedom and self-determination, has become the site of its greatest struggle. The ultimate question we must confront is whether we can reclaim sovereignty over our own minds whether we can break free from the manufactured desires, manipulated identities, and pre-packaged beliefs that have come to define modern life. This is no small task. It requires a radical re-engagement with the principles of critical thinking, an active resistance against the forces that seek to shape our desires, and a collective commitment to the creation of a more autonomous, self-determined society. The battle for freedom, in the final analysis, is not a struggle for political or economic power; it is a struggle for control over the mind itself.

Twenty five

The Unseen Hand: The Quiet Revolution of Corporatocracy

In the age of globalization, where borders blur and ideologies converge, one force stands above all others in its subtle dominion over the world: corporatocracy. This term, often dismissed as hyperbole, is in fact the defining structure of modern power a system where corporate interests, far from merely influencing policy, dictate the contours of political, economic, and social life. Beneath the veneer of democracy, the corporate elite has woven an intricate web of control, exerting influence over not just markets, but the very mechanisms of governance itself.

At first glance, the state may appear to function as the sovereign power, its elected officials the arbiters of public will. Yet, this simplistic view fails to account for the invisible forces that shape policy from the shadows. What has emerged is not a state-run by the people, but one run by those with the means to sway its direction: the global corporate titans. With vast reserves of capital and a global reach that transcends national boundaries, these entities have cultivated a unique form of power asymmetry one in which governments are often beholden to corporate agendas rather than the needs of their own citizens.

The insidious nature of corporatocracy lies in its ability to maintain the illusion of democratic legitimacy while quietly consolidating power behind closed doors. This quiet revolution does not involve tanks in the streets or violent coups. Instead, it operates through the manipulation of policy, the funding of electoral campaigns, and the strategic placement of executives in positions of influence. Corporate lobbying, often dismissed as a mere transactional activity, has become the primary conduit through which policy is crafted. Political decisions whether on environmental regulations, tax policies, or labor laws are shaped by the interests of a few, with the well-being of the many relegated to the margins.

Moreover, this corporatocratic order thrives on complicit silence. The mechanisms of control are so pervasive, so deeply embedded in the fabric of society, that resistance seems futile. Economic institutions, educational systems, and even cultural norms are designed to perpetuate the dominance of corporate interests, creating a reality in which questioning the status quo is not only dangerous but inconceivable. The public, often distracted by manufactured crises or entertainment-driven narratives, remains unaware of the deeper forces at play. And even when awareness arises, the complexity and scale of the system render it nearly impossible to challenge.

This corporate domination is further amplified by the rise of global supply chains and offshoring. The movement of capital across borders has created a situation in which sovereignty is undermined not by foreign invasion, but by the silent migration of wealth and power. Governments, instead of protecting the interests of their citizens, have become facilitators of corporate expansion, offering tax breaks, deregulation, and cheap labor in exchange for investment. The erosion of local economies and the decline of manufacturing industries are but symptoms of a greater malady:

the growing impotence of national governments in the face of corporate might.

The emergence of digital monopolies has further entrenched this corporatocratic order. Tech giants, with their vast reach and control over information, have become not only economic entities but political actors in their own right. They shape public discourse, monitor behavior, and determine the flow of information, all while operating with little accountability. Their influence extends beyond the marketplace, as they play an outsized role in shaping public opinion, dictating cultural trends, and influencing elections. In a world where data is the new gold, these companies have accrued power unprecedented in human history.

Ultimately, the rise of corporatocracy marks the triumph of oligarchical collectivism—a system where a few, through sophisticated mechanisms of control, dictate the terms of existence for the many. Sovereign nations may still exist in form, but their substance is hollowed out, reduced to the role of facilitators for corporate hegemony. This is not a battle of ideologies; it is a struggle for the very control of society's future, one that will determine whether genuine democracy and collective self-determination can survive in an age where the corporate elite reign supreme.

The challenge, then, is not to defeat an enemy that wears a uniform or parades its banner openly. It is to dismantle the systems of power that have become so entrenched and normalized that they are invisible to most. To do so requires a fundamental rethinking of what power is, where it resides, and how it can be reclaimed. The true revolution is not one of violent overthrow but of collective awareness recognizing the systems that shape our world and confronting them with the force of a unified, enlightened public.

Twenty six

The Alchemy of Control: How The Fabric of Society is Woven With Threads of Deception

In the grand tapestry of human civilization, the threads of deception are woven so intricately that their presence becomes invisible to the naked eye. What we perceive as the natural order the structure of society, its norms, its values are, in truth, constructed realities designed to maintain control. At the heart of this controlled narrative lies a sophisticated alchemy, where the base elements of culture, ideology, and economy are transmuted into a potent brew that ensures compliance, stifles dissent, and preserves the dominion of a few. The true architects of this world are not those who wield visible power, but the invisible entities that manipulate the forces of perception, desire, and belief.

This alchemy, though centuries in the making, reaches its zenith in the modern age. Gone are the crude instruments of force and coercion that characterized earlier epochs. Today, power is no longer exerted through overt domination, but through the subtle art of manufacturing consent. The ability to shape the collective consciousness, to influence what people believe is true, what they desire, and how they perceive their own agency, has become the ultimate tool of control. It is not enough to control the actions of the masses; one must first control their thoughts.

The mechanism of this control is found in the interplay of information and illusion. Information, in the modern world, is the most valuable commodity more powerful than gold, more enduring than any currency. And yet, it is also the most malleable. Through a careful orchestration of media narratives, educational structures, and entertainment, the public is subjected to a continuous stream of curated information designed not to inform, but to reshape perception. This is not the free flow of ideas; it is the systematic cultivation of a worldview a worldview that serves the interests of the few by distorting reality and obscuring the truth.

Consider, for example, the manipulation of history. The past, as it is taught to us, is a carefully edited version of events, one that omits the inconvenient truths and glorifies the narratives that legitimize the present order. History, in this sense, becomes not a reflection of the past, but a tool for controlling the future. It is not the record of human struggle and triumph, but a mechanism for creating a sense of inevitability. The story of progress the idea that humanity is moving toward a more enlightened, just, and equitable future becomes a powerful myth that justifies the status quo. The alchemy lies in transforming human suffering and exploitation into a narrative of advancement, where those who have profited from the suffering of others are cast as the "heroes" of history.

This same alchemy extends to the economic system. Capitalism, in its most refined form, does not merely operate as an economic system it is a belief system, a framework for understanding the world, a philosophy of inequality dressed in the language of freedom and choice. It is a system that obscures the mechanisms of exploitation by reframing them as acts of individual agency. The individual, we are told, is the master of their own fate, the architect of their success or failure. But this narrative is a smokescreen, a sleight of hand designed to deflect attention away from the systemic forces that perpetuate inequality. The most insidious aspect of capitalism is its ability to create the illusion of meritocracy the idea that success is purely the result of individual effort, that the winners are simply those who have earned it. This myth diverts attention from the structural forces the exploitation of labor, the concentration of wealth, the manipulation of markets that ensure the persistence of inequality.

The key to maintaining control is the creation of a false sense of freedom. Democracy, once a symbol of liberty, has been recast as a mere spectacle a performance in which citizens play the role of active participants, while the true decisions are made in the backrooms of power. Elections, which should be the ultimate expression of popular will, are reduced to a process of selecting between preordained choices, all of which serve the same vested interests. The veneer of democracy is carefully maintained by the illusion of choice, while the substance of democracy the power to shape one's own future is systematically stripped away. In this grand theater, the public is lulled into a false sense of agency, while the true levers of power remain firmly in the hands of the elite.

But it is not just through information and illusion that this system operates. It also thrives through desire. The alchemy of control is most potent when it taps into the deepest recesses of the human psyche into our desires, our insecurities, and our fears. Modern consumer culture, with its incessant bombardment of advertisements and media, does not simply promote the consumption of goods; it promotes the consumption of identity. Through the purchase of goods, people are sold not just material objects, but the idea of becoming. The aspirational lifestyle the perfect body, the perfect home, the perfect life is sold as a product, a commodity to be acquired. But this idealized version of selfhood is a chimera, a mere projection of a reality that does not exist. Yet, millions are ensnared by it, forever chasing an elusive dream that can never be realized.

This engineered desire is what keeps the wheels of the economic machine turning. The consumption of goods, which appears to be an exercise in personal choice and freedom, is, in fact, a deeply controlled act. The desire to consume is not born naturally; it is implanted, cultivated, and nurtured by an ever-expanding network of influence. Advertisements do not simply sell products; they sell the promise of transformation. The very act of consumption becomes synonymous with self-actualization, reinforcing the idea that true freedom is found in the acquisition of more, in the relentless pursuit of material success.

Yet, for all its seeming invincibility, this alchemical system of control is vulnerable. The threads of illusion, once woven into the fabric of society, are fragile. The more they are stretched, the more they begin to unravel. The truth long buried beneath layers of deception has a way of emerging, often in the most unexpected of ways. And when it does, the whole edifice of control begins to crack. People, once lulled into passivity, begin to see the puppet strings, the manipulation, the forces that have shaped their lives. This awakening is not just a political or economic shift; it is a profound existential rupture. The realization that one has been living within an illusion, that one's life has been molded by forces beyond one's awareness, is a moment of immense power. It is the moment when the alchemist's potion begins to lose its potency, when the veil is lifted, and when true liberation becomes possible.

To challenge this alchemy, then, is not merely to confront a system of wealth or governance; it is to confront the very foundations of perception itself. The battle is not for more power, but for the power to perceive to see the world as it truly is, and not as it has been carefully constructed to appear. It is a battle for the freedom of the mind, for the autonomy of thought, and for the reclamation of one's own desires from the hands of those who would seek to control them. Only then can the alchemical spell of control be broken, and the world be remade on the terms of its true creators: the people.

Twenty seven

The Tyranny of the Status Quo: How Comfort and Complacency Sustain the System

At the crux of modern society lies an insidious force: the tyranny of the status quo. It is a subtle yet unyielding force, not wielded by any single tyrant or government, but by the collective inertia of a system that has come to favor stability over progress, comfort over change, and conformity over rebellion. In a world where discomfort is the exception and ease is the rule, the very desire for a better future is suffocated by the allure of the present. We have come to mistake the absence of chaos for peace, the maintenance of order for justice, and the perpetuation of the existing system for the advancement of society.

The status quo, for all its apparent ordinariness, is a deeply revolutionary force. Its power does not lie in its overt coercion, but in its ability to bind the collective imagination, to paralyze the will to change, and to create a world in which any alternative to the current order feels unthinkable. The true brilliance of the status quo is that it disguises itself as the natural order of things, as if it were an immutable law of nature. This self-sustaining illusion renders resistance nearly impossible, as the very structure of society operates as both the cause and effect of this conformity.

In many ways, this comfort paradox is a consequence of the remarkable success of capitalist modernity. It has seduced us into believing that happiness is found in the accumulation of material goods, in the pursuit of personal pleasure, and in the assurance of individual security. The market, with its insatiable appetite for consumption, has shaped our desires in such a way that we no longer long for freedom in its truest sense, but for more. The capitalist promise is no longer to elevate human existence, but to enhance it with endless commodities that offer transient satisfaction. Yet in this pursuit of more, the most essential thing freedom is lost.

The compulsion to consume is perhaps the most powerful mechanism of control in modern society. From the moment we wake to the moment we sleep, we are presented with an endless array of choices, all designed to make us feel like free agents in a world of infinite possibilities. But in reality, these choices are circumscribed within the narrow confines of the system. The illusion of autonomy is maintained by a constant cycle of distraction, acquisition, and consumption. The result is a populace trapped in a perpetual state of yearning, yet never fulfilled never free from the endless demands of the system that keeps them bound in its orbit.

What sustains this system is not just material wealth, but the psychic economy it has created. The psychic economy refers to the invisible machinery that drives individuals to internalize the values of the status quo, to identify their self-worth with their purchasing power, and to equate success with consumption. In this economy, identity is not forged through collective struggle or shared purpose, but through the perpetual acquisition of status-signifying goods, experiences, and identities. The result is a population that is atomized, individualized, and disconnected from the larger forces that shape their lives. The more one consumes, the more one is made to feel whole but this wholeness is an illusion, a hollow shell that conceals the profound alienation that defines modern existence.

This psychic economy is further perpetuated by the mechanisms of media and advertising, which serve as the dual engines that fuel both the desire for material wealth and the justification for the existing order. The advertisements that bombard us daily are not simply selling products they are selling identities, narratives, and ways of being. These ads create a world where our worth is measured by what we own, what we wear, and where we live. They craft a vision of success that is intrinsically tied to consumption and individualism, and by doing so, they reinforce the very structures that perpetuate inequality and exploitation.

The opium of comfort is, however, not confined to the individual realm. It extends its reach into the political domain, where the rhetoric of incrementalism and the promise of small, manageable reforms serve as the opiate for a society that craves stability over revolution. The political establishment, rather than challenging the fundamental inequities of the system, offers up piecemeal solutions that do little more than placate the masses. These reforms are carefully calibrated to maintain the illusion of progress, to assure the public that their concerns are being addressed, while in reality, they serve to reinforce the very power structures that keep society in its current, unequal state.

Even when faced with crisis, the status quo adapts to maintain its grip on power. Economic downturns, environmental catastrophes, social unrest all of these can be repackaged as opportunities for greater control. The very system that causes the crises is the one that offers the "solution" to them, thus reinforcing its legitimacy. In times of disaster, the public is told that only the system—whether it be corporations, governments, or the financial elite—has the resources and the expertise to steer society out of peril. This rhetoric of "stability" in the face of chaos becomes a powerful tool for quashing revolutionary impulses and maintaining the structure of power.

The comfort paradox is most evident in the way society responds to the specter of change. When confronted with the possibility of transformation whether through revolutionary politics, radical economic reform, or societal upheaval there is a profound collective fear of the unknown. Even those who are oppressed by the system often hesitate to break free, for the status quo, with all its flaws, is familiar. It offers a sense of security, a sense of order, and the reassurance that, for all its injustices, it is at least predictable. Change, by contrast, is perceived as chaos a destabilizing force that could unravel the very fabric of society. The result is a collective paralysis, a resistance to change that is fueled not by rational thought, but by a deep-seated fear of losing the comfort of the known.

But this complacency, this malaise of comfort, is not inevitable. It is a constructed condition, one that can be undone by a fundamental shift in how we understand freedom, identity, and the purpose of human life. To break free from the tyranny of the status quo, one must first recognize its existence not just in the external world of politics and economics, but in the internal world of self-perception and desire. True freedom lies not in the accumulation of goods or the promise of security, but in the courage to question, to resist, and to imagine new possibilities beyond the constraints of the system. Only then can the comfort that binds us be transformed into the power that liberates.

Twenty eight

The Echoes of Empire: How History's Ghosts Continue to Shape Our Present

History, with its mythologies and narratives, is often viewed as a linear progression, a series of events that lead us toward an ever-more enlightened future. We are told that the past is behind us, its lessons learned, its mistakes rectified, its injustices redressed. Yet, in truth, the past is never gone. It lingers in the shadows, its ghosts haunting our present, subtly shaping the contours of our reality in ways both profound and imperceptible. The echoes of empire, long after the empires themselves have crumbled, continue to reverberate through the corridors of power, resounding in the structures of inequality, domination, and exploitation that govern our lives today.

The notion of empire an institution of vast power and unchecked authority has evolved over time. In the ancient world, it took the form of territorial conquest, the subjugation of entire peoples, and the imposition of cultural hegemony. In the modern era, however, empire has become more disembodied, no longer confined to physical borders but extending its reach into the globalized networks of trade, finance, and information. The imperial project is no longer defined by the direct control of land, but by the ability to control the flow of capital, the shaping of ideologies, and the manipulation of global narratives.

The modern world, despite its insistence on post-imperial progress, remains a neocolonial system, in which the legacy of empire continues to dictate the terms of existence for billions of people. The financialized world order, driven by transnational corporations, international financial institutions, and a class of global elites, mirrors the structure of empire in ways both obvious and insidious. Just as the great empires of the past extracted resources from their colonies to fuel their own prosperity, the modern capitalist system thrives on the extraction of wealth from the Global South, the exploitation of cheap labor, and the plunder of natural resources.

The empire, in its new guise, is not an entity bound by the visible trappings of nation-states, but a transnational network of power that transcends borders. This empire operates through the mechanisms of debt, the architecture of global trade, and the digital apparatus that connects the world's financial markets. It is not a visible monarchy or an occupying army that maintains control, but an invisible web of interconnected systems, ideologies, and interests that legitimize inequality on a global scale. In this new empire, the true rulers are not kings or presidents, but the faceless institutions banks, corporations, and international organizations that dictate the terms of existence for the majority of humanity.

At the heart of this modern empire lies a paradox: the more interconnected and "civilized" the world becomes, the more entrenched and invisible the mechanisms of domination become. Empires of the past may have been brutal in their overt control, but today's empire is far more sophisticated, far more insidious. It cloaks itself in the language of progress, democracy, and freedom, while perpetuating systems of control that are more subtle, more pervasive, and ultimately more difficult to dismantle. This modern imperialism is not based on territorial conquest or military might, but on the control of information, the manipulation of markets, and the systematic reordering of social relations to serve the interests of a small, global elite.

The persistence of these imperial echoes is felt most acutely in the very structures of global finance. Just as empires of old extracted wealth from colonies through the imposition of taxes, tariffs, and labor systems, so too does the contemporary financial system extract wealth from the global poor through mechanisms such as debt traps, austerity measures, and neoliberal economic policies. The vast accumulation of wealth in the hands of a few is not the result of individual merit or innovation, but the byproduct of a system that systematically transfers resources from the Global South to the Global North. The international debt system, in particular, has become a modern-day chain, binding countries to the whims of international lenders and perpetuating cycles of poverty, inequality, and political instability.

In the realm of culture, the legacy of empire persists through the imposition of Western values, ideologies, and norms upon the rest of the world. The global cultural hegemony, driven by the dominance of Western media, corporations, and educational systems, seeks to homogenize the diverse expressions of human existence, replacing indigenous knowledge systems, languages, and ways of life with those defined by the global elite. This cultural imperialism operates not through violent conquest, but through the subtle appropriation of local cultures and traditions, transforming them into commodities that can be consumed, marketed, and sold. The process is so pervasive that it becomes invisible, and those who resist it are often made to feel backward, primitive, or obsolete.

Moreover, the intellectual heirs of empire continue to shape the world through the philosophies of domination that underpin modern political and economic systems. The neoliberal worldview, with its emphasis on individualism, free markets, and minimal government intervention, is not a product of some natural, inevitable progression in human thought; it is the legacy of an imperial mindset that views the world in terms of hierarchies and dominance. The very language of neoliberalism the language of competition, efficiency, and "market forces" mimics the rhetoric of empire, which has always sought to divide the world into rulers and ruled, masters and servants. At its core, neoliberalism is a philosophy of imperialism: the idea that a few should control the resources and opportunities of the many, that wealth should flow upwards, and that the majority should remain subjugated to the whims of a tiny, all-powerful elite.

The ghosts of empire also linger in the form of nationalism, which, despite its surface-level appeal to self-determination, often serves as a distraction from the deeper, more insidious forces of global domination. Nationalism, in its modern iteration, is frequently manipulated by elites to maintain control over the populace, to create the illusion of sovereignty while the true sources of power lie beyond national borders. It encourages the populace to focus on artificial divisions between nations, races, and religions, while obscuring the fact that global capitalism the true engine of modern imperialism operates beyond national boundaries. Nationalism, in this sense, serves as a smokescreen for the continuation of imperial domination, deflecting attention away from the ways in which global power structures are being used to perpetuate inequality, exploitation, and violence.

The continued prevalence of empire's influence is perhaps most clearly visible in the global military-industrial complex, which, despite the end of formal colonialism, still maintains a vast and intrusive presence in many parts of the world. The mechanisms of empire may have evolved, but the desire to control, dominate, and exploit remains unchanged. The military apparatus that extends across the globe, with its vast network of bases, technologies, and alliances, ensures that the empire's interests are safeguarded at any cost. From the pacification of dissenting populations to the protection of resource-rich regions, the modern empire's military is a global enforcer of economic and political stability, ensuring that the flow of capital, resources, and wealth is uninterrupted.

To truly understand the nature of this modern empire and to dismantle its power one must first recognize the continuity between the past and the present. The empire is not an artifact of history, nor a relic of a bygone age. It is a living system, one that evolves and adapts to the changing tides of time, always seeking new ways to maintain its dominance. The illusion of a post-imperial world is just that: an illusion. The empire's ghosts are still with us, and until we acknowledge their presence and confront their legacy, we will remain trapped in the chains they have forged.

Only by confronting the deep structures of power that continue to sustain these imperial echoes whether in the form of global finance, cultural hegemony, or military dominance can we hope to break free from their influence. True freedom, true liberation, lies in our ability to unmask these structures, to expose the ways in which they operate, and to build a new world order that prioritizes equality, justice, and solidarity over domination and control. The ghosts of empire may still haunt us, but they need not define.

Twenty nine

The Threshold of Awakening: A World on the Edge

The journey through these pages has, no doubt, carried us to the very edge of understanding perhaps even to the precipice of a new consciousness. In our quest to dissect the hidden forces of power, wealth, and corruption, we have uncovered the grand, yet often invisible, architectures that have shaped our world. From the illusory narratives of virtue to the shadowy agents of control, we have, in many ways, dismantled the façades that have long concealed the true nature of the systems that govern us. But in this final moment of reckoning, it is crucial to ask: what lies beyond this awareness? What is the cost of this illumination, and what will we do with the knowledge we have gained?

For knowledge, like fire, can be both a liberator and a destroyer. It has the power to ignite revolution, to dismantle empires, to shatter chains. But it also has the capacity to burn, to blind, to overwhelm.

The question we now face is whether we will allow the light of truth to illuminate the path forward, or whether we will be consumed by the very flames we have kindled. The threshold of awakening—the moment at which we first see the world as it truly is—requires more than just understanding; it demands action, responsibility, and an irrevocable choice: to walk through the door of change, or to retreat into the comforting shadows of denial.

In the wake of this awakening, we must confront the staggering complexity of the world we inhabit. For all its grandeur and apparent simplicity, the system we face is anything but monolithic. It is a tangled web, a shifting mosaic of competing forces and contradictions. Even within the very structures of affluence, power, and privilege that we have so carefully dissected, there are fractures, fissures, and openings that can be exploited for transformation. But transformation is never easy, and it is certainly not without cost. The question now is not whether change is possible, but whether we are willing to embrace it to confront the unknown, to face the personal and collective sacrifices that are required to dismantle the systems of domination that have so thoroughly embedded themselves in our consciousness.

The forces of wealth and power do not simply act as external agents of oppression they are, in many respects, a reflection of our own inner conflicts. They are the outward manifestations of the fear and desire that drive human behavior: fear of scarcity, fear of loss, fear of insignificance; and desire for comfort, security, recognition, and control. These forces are not abstract concepts; they are woven into the very fabric of our psyches, into the very ways in which we interact with one another and the world around us. This makes the work of transformation infinitely more difficult, for it is not simply a matter of overthrowing external systems, but of confronting the internalized beliefs that perpetuate those systems. The empire of wealth and power exists not only in the boardrooms and palaces of the elite, but in the quiet, often unnoticed corners of our own minds, where the seeds of complacency, apathy, and self-interest are sown.

To break free from this empire requires not only an external revolution, but a radical shift in consciousness a breaking apart of the false identities and narratives that bind us to the status quo. It is not enough to acknowledge the existence of injustice; we must also reject the ideologies that justify it. We must, in essence, deconstruct the very foundations upon which our current understanding of success, wealth, and power rests. And this deconstruction is a painful process, for it demands that we strip away the comforts and securities that have long been a part of our identity. It requires that we confront our own complicity in the systems of oppression, even as we seek to dismantle them.

This moment of reckoning is, therefore, a moment of profound ambiguity of being caught between the world that we know and the world that we must create. The old systems are crumbling, but the new systems are not yet fully formed. We are at a precipice, poised between the known and the unknown, between what has been and what could be. In this moment, we are confronted with the terrifying and exhilarating possibility that we may be the architects of the future. But to build a new world, we must first deconstruct the old one not just externally, but within ourselves. We must confront the narratives, the assumptions, and the beliefs that have shaped our understanding of reality, and we must be willing to replace them with something more just, more inclusive, and more equitable.

It is here, at the threshold of this awakening, that we must ask ourselves: what is our role in this moment? Will we allow the tides of history to wash over us, as passive spectators, or will we seize this moment to reshape the currents of change? The empire we face is not solely one of wealth, power, and corruption; it is also an empire of ideas, of values, of beliefs. If we are to overcome it, we must first overcome the empire within our own internalized beliefs about what is possible, about what is just, about what it means to live a good life. We must be willing to question, to challenge, and to disrupt the very foundations of our thinking, our living, and our being.

This is the essence of revolutionary thought: to recognize that everything we know is subject to revision, to questioning, to transformation. And yet, as we venture further into this unknown territory, we must also confront a paradox. For in seeking to dismantle the systems of domination and oppression, we are not merely fighting against an external force we are also fighting against our own human nature. The desire for power, for security, for recognition, is not something that is imposed upon us from the outside. It is part of our DNA, part of the human condition. And so, the struggle for liberation is, in many ways, a struggle against ourselves against our own fears, our own desires, and our own capacity for complacency.

This is where the true work of revolution lies not in the grand gestures of resistance, but in the small, daily acts of transformation that begin within each of us. To change the world, we must first change ourselves. To liberate the oppressed, we must first liberate our own hearts and minds. To break free from the chains of domination, we must first break free from the narratives of power and control that have shaped our very consciousness.

In this final reckoning, we must ask ourselves: what kind of world do we want to build? What kind of legacy do we wish to leave behind? The power to shape the future lies not in the hands of a few, but in the collective will of those who dare to awaken, to see the world as it truly is, and to act in accordance with that vision. It is a power that resides not in the hands of governments or corporations, but in the hands of every individual who refuses to remain silent, who refuses to accept the status quo, and who dares to imagine a different world a world of justice, of equity, of compassion, and of true freedom.

In the end, the revolution is not just about toppling the external empires of wealth and power. It is about dismantling the empire within, and in doing so, creating a new reality one that is not bound by the chains of fear, greed, and inequality, but one that is grounded in love, in justice, and in the recognition of our shared humanity.

The Reckoning of Silence: Confronting the Empire Within

As we arrive at the closing pages of this examination, we are compelled to ask what, exactly, have we uncovered? What, if anything, does it mean to unearth the tangled web of wealth, malfeasance, and systemic oppression that runs through the veins of our world? What is the ultimate purpose of shining light on the forces of affluence and domination that have shaped and continue to shape the fate of billions? Knowledge when properly harnessed can be a potent weapon against tyranny, yet knowledge alone is insufficient. It may expose, but it does not always liberate. The question that haunts us now is whether this unveiling of the hidden architectures of power will lead to action or merely to further complacency. In seeking to expose the deeper currents of affluence and malfeasance, have we merely pointed to the abyss, or are we calling for its collapse?

In these pages, I have dissected the mirage of virtue that masks the true nature of wealth, the subterranean forces that manipulate global systems from the shadows, the illusory freedoms we are sold, and the tangled web of imperial legacies that continue to define our modern political and economic realities. But if the pages of this book have merely ended with the identification of problems, then we have failed to engage in the most crucial part of the process: the reckoning. For in unveiling the corrupt mechanisms of the world, there lies an even deeper, more insidious force a force so subtle, so deeply ingrained in our collective consciousness, that its very existence remains unchallenged by most. This force is the empire within.

The world we inhabit is not merely shaped by the external forces of wealth and power that operate in boardrooms or political capitals. It is shaped by the quiet, invisible empire that resides within the very recesses of our own minds. It is an empire not of soldiers and statesmen, but of thoughts, of beliefs, of assumptions assumptions that dictate how we view the world and our place in it. It is an empire of silence, an empire of complacency the inner machinery that binds us to a system of inequality, of exploitation, and of environmental degradation. The very act of accepting the status quo is the most profound act of subjugation. We are not simply controlled by external powers, we are complicit in our own enslavement, consenting to the invisible chains that have been forged within our psyches.

The tragedy of the empire within is that it goes unnoticed. We are taught to focus on the visible markers of power on the heads of state, on the institutions of corporate governance, on the seemingly omnipotent figures who appear to shape the world. And yet, beneath these visible structures lies the invisible empire of norms, values, and beliefs that shape our daily lives. This empire is not built on force, but on influence a far more potent and insidious form of control. It is the quiet persuasion that convinces us to accept a world of exploitation as normal, that transforms inequality into inevitability. It tells us that we are powerless, that the structures of power are too vast to challenge, that our individual actions do not matter in the grand scheme of things. It convinces us to remain silent in the face of injustice and to accept the injustices that permeate our world as natural, as part of the inevitable order of things.

The invisible empire is the empire of complacency of acceptance. It thrives on our desire for comfort, our need for security, and our fear of the unknown. To challenge the system, to confront the vast forces of oppression and exploitation that govern our lives, is to enter into discomfort to reject the status quo, to reject the narrative that has been fed to us, and to see the world as it truly is, not as we have been taught to see it. This is the work of the revolutionary: to disrupt the internalized narratives of dominance and to break free from the prison of thought that sustains the empire. It is not enough to call out the corrupt structures of power from the outside; we must also confront the ways in which we have internalized those structures, the ways in which we have learned to see the world through the lens of hierarchy, of domination, of inequality.

This process of internal reckoning is not a passive one. It is an active, ongoing practice of unlearning, of breaking free from the chains that we have forged ourselves. The journey of liberation begins in the mind. It begins with a willingness to question to question not only the system in which we live, but the very assumptions that underlie our understanding of that system. It begins with the realization that the empire within is not natural, it is not inevitable, but that it has been constructed through centuries of cultural, political, and economic processes designed to ensure our compliance. Once we recognize this fact, once we understand that the very system of domination is a product of human design, we begin to realize that it can also be dismantled.

But dismantling the empire within is not a task for the faint of heart. It requires a radical act of self-awareness and self-reflection a willingness to confront the dissonance between what we know and what we accept. It requires a recognition that true freedom is not simply the absence of external oppression, but the presence of internal liberation. This is the work of revolution not the kind that comes from the barrel of a gun or the collapse of governments, but the kind that arises from within the individual, from within the collective consciousness. It is a revolution of thought, of awareness, of will. It is the kind of revolution that begins in small, daily actions the refusal to accept injustice, the questioning of narratives that have been fed to us, the decision to reject the comfort of silence in favor of the discomfort of truth.

The empire within is sustained by a deeply embedded psychic economy. This economy operates not in terms of dollars and cents, but in terms of emotional capital. We are trained to value comfort, security, and predictability over risk, uncertainty, and change. The dominant culture feeds us the narrative that our value lies in our ability to maintain our place in the system to climb the ladder, to consume more, to fit into the mold that has been created for us. The system rewards those who play by its rules and punishes those who deviate from the norm. But in this system of rewards and punishments, we lose sight of the most fundamental truth: that the greatest act of resistance is not in climbing the ladder, but in refusing to play the game.

The true act of rebellion, the most profound act of liberation, is not in overthrowing the external powers that seek to control us, but in liberating ourselves from the internal forces that keep us bound to the system. It is in the refusal to accept the false narratives of success, of power, of progress, that have been fed to us. It is in the unlearning of the patterns of behavior and thought that sustain the empire. Only then can we begin to create new, more just systems of living, of being, and of relating to one another. These new systems will not arise through grandiose gestures or violent upheavals, but through the small, daily acts of resistance that emerge from a deep-seated awareness of our collective power and interconnectedness.

The greatest paradox of the empire within is that it thrives on illusion. It thrives on our belief that we are separate, that we are isolated, that we have no power. The empire within tells us that we are insignificant, that we are powerless, that change is impossible. But the truth is that the empire itself is a fabrication a construction, a lie told to us by the very forces that seek to control us. The most revolutionary act is simply to see the world as it truly is and to act in accordance with that vision.

Thus, as we come to the conclusion of this exploration, let us not dwell only on the external forces of affluence, malfeasance, and empire. Let us also turn our gaze inward, to confront the empire that resides within us all. Let us acknowledge that we are both the prisoners and the prison—the architects and the inhabitants of the world we live in. Only by confronting and dismantling the empire within can we hope to create a world that is truly free.

This is the work that lies ahead. This is the revolution we must all undertake each of us, in our own way, in our own time. And in this work, we will find our liberation not in grand gestures or spectacular victories, but in the quiet, persistent revolution of our thoughts, our actions, and our collective will.

The Labyrinth of Self Awakening to the Infinite

In the grand, unfolding narrative of existence, there comes a moment often imperceptible to the untrained eye when the vastness of the world we inhabit reveals itself in full measure. This moment, this awakening, is not always a singular event, but rather the culmination of a quiet tension that has been building over a lifetime, a pulse that grows stronger with each passing moment, each new insight, and each new rupture in the seamless fabric of our perceptions. It is in this moment, perhaps as you turn the final pages of this book, that you stand at the threshold of a new understanding—not just of the world, but of yourself.

For all the dissection of power, corruption, and wealth that we have traversed in this journey, there remains one unyielding truth: the most formidable empire the one that has shaped every other is the empire of the self. It is here, within the labyrinth of our consciousness, that the deepest forms of control are exercised. It is within this internal dominion that the seeds of complacency, subjugation, and acceptance of the status quo are sown. For no matter how vast the structures of power that we expose no matter how insidious the forces of wealth and domination they are but external manifestations of the empire we have cultivated within.

The tyranny of the self is the quietest of tyrants, for it operates with the consent of its subjects. It feeds on the very ideas we hold about who we are, what we are capable of, and how we fit into the world. It thrives on our most basic fears fear of inadequacy, fear of failure, fear of being unworthy. It shapes our desires desires for validation, for success, for acceptance and in doing so, it molds our choices, our actions, and ultimately, our lives. And yet, it is within the interior of this self-made prison that the potential for true freedom resides.

We speak of revolution, of dismantling the vast structures of power that shape our world, and rightly so. These structures are corrupt, exploitative, and antithetical to the principles of justice and equality. But the first revolution the one that must precede all others is the revolution of the mind. It is the awakening to the fact that the greatest chains we carry are not those forged by external powers, but those that we willingly accept, internalize, and perpetuate within our own psyche. These chains bind us to the narratives of limitation, of powerlessness, of fear, and of acceptance. It is the rejection of these narratives that constitutes the first step toward genuine liberation.

Consider, for a moment, the nature of freedom itself. True freedom is not merely the absence of external oppression, nor the ability to make choices within a given system. It is the liberation of the mind, the ability to transcend the limitations that we have internalized, and to perceive the world and ourselves in its infinite potential. It is the recognition that the world is not bound by the systems of power that exist today, but by the stories we tell ourselves about what is possible. These stories are not the province of governments, corporations, or institutions; they are the constructs of our own making. The moment we awaken to this fact, we unlock the true potential of human agency.

The journey toward awakening is fraught with difficulty, for the self is not easily confronted. It is not simply a matter of recognizing the external systems of oppression and malfeasance; it is the far more subtle task of recognizing the ways in which we, too, have become complicit in our own subjugation. We have internalized the stories of scarcity, of competition, of hierarchy, and of domination. We have accepted the notion that power, wealth, and status are the ultimate measures of worth, and in doing so, we have allowed ourselves to be molded by the very forces we claim to oppose.

To break free from this internal empire is not a task for the faint of heart. It requires an unwavering commitment to self-examination, to the disruption of the stories we have told ourselves about who we are, and to the dismantling of the false identities we have assumed in order to survive in a world that prizes compliance over creativity, conformity over individuality. It is a journey that begins with a simple, yet profound, act of courage: the willingness to question everything. To ask, "What is true?" not in the abstract sense, but in the most intimate and personal sense. What is true about my life, my choices, my values? What is true about the way I relate to the world, to others, and to myself?

This journey is not linear. It is not a simple matter of turning a page and stepping into a new world. It is a process of continuous discovery and unbecoming. With every revelation comes a deeper level of awareness, but also a greater confrontation with the shadows within us. It is easy to look outward and blame the forces of wealth, power, and corruption for the injustices we face. It is far more difficult to look inward and acknowledge the ways in which we, too, have contributed to the perpetuation of those same systems. But it is this inward turn the willingness to confront the empire of the self that holds the key to true liberation.

The question then becomes: what will we do with this knowledge? How will we, as individuals and as a collective, respond to the awakening that is unfolding within us? Will we turn away from it, back into the comforting shadows of ignorance and denial? Or will we embrace it, despite the discomfort, despite the disillusionment, and walk through the threshold into the unknown?

True revolution does not come from the overthrow of governments or the dismantling of institutions. It begins in the smallest of spaces the interior of the self. To change the world, we must first change the way we see it. We must relinquish the notion that we are bound by the forces of external power, and recognize that we are the architects of our own reality. The power to transform the world lies not in the hands of the few who hold wealth and influence, but in the hearts and minds of the many who choose, each day, to awaken from their slumber and embrace the infinite possibilities that lie before them.

It is not enough to understand the systems of oppression that govern our world. We must also confront the systems of oppression that govern our minds. We must liberate ourselves from the false beliefs and limitations that bind us to a world of scarcity, competition, and domination. We must rise above the narratives of fear and scarcity that have been ingrained in us and embrace a new story a story of abundance, of connection, and of possibility. And as we do, we will find that the world around us begins to shift, not because of the actions of the few, but because of the collective will of those who have chosen, through their own awakening, to see the world anew.

In this moment of transition, we stand at the edge of infinite potential. But it is up to each of us individually and collectively to step forward, to leave behind the comforts of the known, and to embrace the boundless future that awaits us. The revolution is not external; it is internal. It begins in the mind, and it spreads outward into the world, creating ripples that can alter the very fabric of existence. The choice is ours. The revolution is now.

Chandra, a political science graduate from Delhi University, delves into the intricate mechanisms of power, governance, and societal constructs through his writings with a focus on the pervasive influence of wealth and its entanglement with systemic malfeasance, his work seeks to unravel the less conspicuous but deeply entrenched forces shaping contemporary politics. The Clandestine Politics of Affluence and Malfeasance, the inaugral volume of his ambitious series Sailing Upside Down, embarks on an incisive exhamination of the moral and ethical undercurrents that underpin the consolidation of affluence and authority.

In The Clandestine Politics of Affluence and Malfeasance, the veil over society's most insidious constructs is lifted with unsparing precision. Through a tapestry of erudite analysis and unflinching critique, this work dissects the subversive interplay of wealth, corruption, and the silent machinations that govern human systems. At its heart lies an exploration of affluence as both architect and antagonist an omnipresent force capable of engineering prosperity yet fostering moral decay. The corridors of power, cloaked in secrecy, reveal how malfeasance is not a mere aberration but a calculated companion to privilege. This book is a clarion call for those who dare to navigate the treacherous waters of societal constructs and question the equilibrium of a world sailing precariously upside down. To the discerning reader, it offers intellectual provocation, unearthing truths that refuse to remain buried beneath the weight of influence and denial. Prepare to confront the uncomfortable realities of systems built on illusion, exploitation, and quiet compliance. For in this meticulously crafted expose lies the stark realization: the pursuit of justice is impossible without first understanding the politics of power.